John L. Mies

Gladys Horiuchi

Louis P. Martini

Cambornica

Allen Lewis

(Louis) LATOUR

Robin Kelley O'Connor

Mike Stephens

Alistair Robertson

Marvin R. Shanken

LF Bouchard

Rodney D. Strong

James Trezise

David S. ...

"There are no standards of taste in wine, cigars, poetry, prose, etc. Each man's own taste is the standard, and a majority vote cannot decide for him or in any slightest degree affect the supremacy of his own standard."

—MARK TWAIN, 1895

Kevin Zraly's

◆

WINDOWS ON
THE WORLD

WINE JOURNAL

Kevin Zraly's

WINDOWS ON

THE WORLD

WINE JOURNAL

Kevin Zraly

STERLING INNOVATION
An imprint of Sterling Publishing Co., Inc.

New York / London
www.sterlingpublishing.com

STERLING, the Sterling Logo, STERLING INNOVATION, and the Sterling Innovation
logo are registered trademarks of Sterling Publishing Co., Inc.

2 4 6 8 10 9 7 5 3 1

Published by Sterling Publishing Co., Inc.
387 Park Avenue South, New York, NY 10016

This book is comprised of material from the following title: *Windows on the World Complete Wine Course*

Distributed in Canada by Sterling Publishing
^c/o Canadian Manda Group, 165 Dufferin Street
Toronto, Ontario, Canada M6K 3H6
Distributed in the United Kingdom by GMC Distribution Services
Castle Place, 166 High Street, Lewes, East Sussex, England BN7 1XU
Distributed in Australia by Capricorn Link (Australia) Pty. Ltd.
P.O. Box 704, Windsor, NSW 2756, Australia

Printed in China

Cover image © Elizabeth Watt
Page iv: Image © Alexey Khlobystov, 2009 Used under license from iStockphoto.com
Page 2: Image © Anna Jurkovska, 2009 Used under license from Shutterstock.com
Page 14: Image © Graham Prentice, 2009 Used under license from Shutterstock.com
Page 21: Illustration adapted by permission from Tim Jacob, http://www.cf.ac.uk/biosi/staff/jacob
Page 30: Illustration © Jerome Scholler, 2009 Used under license from Shutterstock.com
Page 40: Image © A. L. Spangler, 2009 Used under license from Shutterstock.com
Page 54: Image © Rafael Garcia, 2009 Used under license from iStockphoto.com
Page 59: Illustration © Francesco Abrignani, 2009 Used under license from Shutterstock.com

Sterling ISBN 978-1-4027-6837-8

For information about custom editions, special sales, premium and
corporate purchases, please contact Sterling Special Sales
Department at 800-805-5489 or specialsales@sterlingpublishing.com.

INTRODUCTION

I BEGAN MY WINE JOURNEY as a nineteen-year-old college student, and like most students, I had a "negative" cash flow. I was lucky to have worked weekends in a fabulous restaurant that had a small, but well selected wine list. The only way for me to learn about wine was to go to as many industry sponsored wine tastings (free) that I could.

They were usually stand up tastings and featured hundreds of different wines. The only way to "survive" these tastings and actually remember the wines the next day was to take copious notes. As a result, I created my own journal, a rating system, and collected labels that I referred back to as I continued my wine studies. I still have those notes and labels today! Having a journal was a great way to follow my wine education and my own taste preferences over the years.

I was extremely happy when my publisher suggested writing a wine journal that would also provide essential information on the basics of wine, how to taste like a pro, and how to store your wines and protect your investment.

We have also added a chapter on great value wines. Every year I taste thousands of wines, always looking for the $20 bottle of wine that tastes like the $50 bottle. Finally, the vintage best bets lists the best years to buy from the different wine regions around the world.

Good luck on your own wine journey!

This book is dedicated to everyone who has a passion for wine, from the grape growers to the winemakers, from the buyer, sellers, and the label designers, to, most importantly, the wine consumers.

May your glass always be more full than empty!

PRODUCE OF FRANCE

MIS EN BOUTEILLE AU CHÂTEAU

GRAND VIN
DE
CHATEAU LATOUR

PREMIER GRAND CRU CLASSÉ

PAUILLAC

1993

12,5 % Vol. 750 ml

DÉPOSÉ APPELLATION PAUILLAC CONTRÔLÉE

STE CIVILE DU VIGNOBLE DE CHATEAU LATOUR, PROPRIETAIRE A PAUILLAC (GIRONDE) · LG 93

Château Cheval Blanc

1er Grand Cru Classé

1996   SPÉCIMEN

St Emilion Grand Cru

APPELLATION SAINT-ÉMILION GRAND CRU CONTRÔLÉE

Mis en bouteille au Château   13 % BY VOL.

St Civile du Cheval Blanc, Hrs Fourcaud-Laussac

PROPRIÉTAIRE A ST-EMILION (GIRONDE) FRANCE   750 ml.

1973, en hommage à Picasso (1881-1973)

PABLO PICASSO · BACCHANALE · MUSÉE DE MOUTON

1973

Château
Mouton Rothschild

PREMIER CRU CLASSÉ EN 1973

PREMIER JE SUIS   SECOND JE FUS
MOUTON NE CHANGE

LE BARON PHILIPPE   PROPRIÉTAIRE
APPELLATION   PAUILLAC   CONTROLÉE
PRODUCT OF FRANCE
73 cl   TOUTE LA RECOLTE MISE EN BOUTEILLES AU CHATEAU

OPUS ONE

A NAPA VALLEY
RED WINE

PRODUCED AND
BOTTLED BY

ROBERT MONDAVI
BARON PHILIPPE DE ROTHSCHILD

OAKVILLE, CALIFORNIA
PRODUCT OF USA
750 ML/75 9 CL
ALCOHOL 13.5% BY VOLUME

RIDGE   2003
CALIFORNIA
GEYSERVILLE®

76% ZINFANDEL, 18% CARIGNANE, 6% PETITE SIRAH
SONOMA COUNTY   14.6% ALCOHOL BY VOLUME
PRODUCED & BOTTLED BY RIDGE VINEYARDS, INC.
17100 MONTE BELLO ROAD, BOX 1810, CUPERTINO, CA 95015

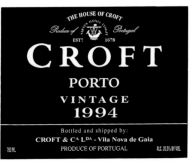

THE HOUSE OF CROFT

Produce of Portugal

EST. 1678

CROFT

PORTO

VINTAGE
1994

Bottled and shipped by:
CROFT & CA LDA - Vila Nova de Gaia
PRODUCE OF PORTUGAL

750 ML   ALC. 20.5% BY VOL.

1995

JOSEPH PHELPS

INSIGNIA

NAPA
VALLEY

RED TABLE WINE · CABERNET SAUVIGNON 90% · MERLOT 7% · PETIT VERDOT 3%

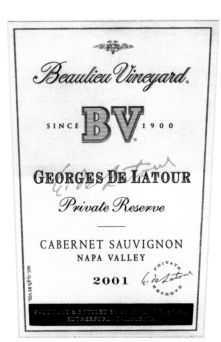

Beaulieu Vineyard.

SINCE 1900

BV.

GEORGES DE LATOUR

Private Reserve

CABERNET SAUVIGNON
NAPA VALLEY

2001

PRODUCED & BOTTLED BY BEAULIEU VINEYARD
RUTHERFORD, CALIFORNIA

GRAND VIN

CHATEAU
LYNCH ✦ BAGES

GRAND CRU CLASSÉ

PAUILLAC

APPELLATION PAUILLAC CONTROLEE

1995   13% vol.

MISE EN BOUTEILLE AU CHÂTEAU

A CAZES Propriétaire a PAUILLAC (Gironde)   300 cl

PRODUCE OF FRANCE

PIO CESARE

ALBA

CASA
FONDATA
NEL
1881

Barolo

DENOMINAZIONE DI ORIGINE CONTROLLATA E GARANTITA

PRODUCED AND BOTTLED IN ITALY BY

Pio Cesare

NET CONTENTS 750 ML.
ALCOHOL 13.5% BY VOL.

RED WINE   ALBA
ITALIA

CONTENTS

PRELUDE
TO WINE

HOW WINE IS MADE

GRAPE VARIETIES AND TYPES OF WINE

VITAL WINE STATISTICS

THE FIVE major wine importers into the United States:
1. France (31%)
2. Italy (28%)
3. Australia (17%)
4. Spain (5.8%)
5. Chile (4.5%)

These 5 countries account for almost 87% of the total value of wine imported into the U.S.

TWENTY-TWO brand names equal 50% of the total wine market.
SOURCE: *Impact Databank*

THE TOP TEN producers of wine in the world:

1. Italy	6. Australia
2. France	7. China
3. Spain	8. South Africa
4. United States	9. Germany
5. Argentina	10. Chile

WINE IS FAT FREE and contains no cholesterol.

WINDOWS ON WINE 2009
World Production - 39 billion bottles
World Consumption - 33 billion bottles
Acres of Vineyards - 19.6 million

TOP 3 IMPORTED wines sold in the U.S.
Yellow Tail (Australia)
Cavit (Italy)
Concha y Toro (Chile)

THE HIGHER the alcohol in a wine, the more body (weight) it will usually have.

ALCOHOL WHEN consumed in moderation will increase HDL (good) and decrease LDL (bad) cholesterol.

A BOTTLE of wine is 86% water.

MORE ACRES of grapes are planted than any other fruit crop in the world!

THE BASICS

You're in a wine shop looking for that "special" wine to serve at a dinner party. Before you walked in, you had at least an idea of what you wanted, but now, as you scan the shelves, you're overwhelmed. "There are so many wines," you think, "and so many prices." You take a deep breath, boldly pick up a bottle that looks impressive, and buy it. Then you hope your guests will like your selection.

Does this sound a little farfetched? For some of you, yes. Yet the truth is, this is a very common occurrence for the wine beginner, and even someone with intermediate wine knowledge, but it doesn't have to be that way. Wine should be an enjoyable experience. By the time you finish this journal, you'll be able to buy with confidence from a retailer or even look in the eyes of a wine steward and ask with no hesitation for the selection of your choice. But first let's start with the basics—the foundation of your wine knowledge.

For the purpose of this book, wine is the fermented juice of grapes.

HOW WINE IS MADE

What's fermentation?

Fermentation is the process by which the grape juice turns into wine. The simple formula for fermentation is:

$$\text{Sugar} + \text{Yeast} = \text{Alcohol} + \text{Carbon Dioxide (CO}_2)$$

The fermentation process begins when the grapes are crushed and ends when all of the sugar has been converted to alcohol or the alcohol level has reached around 15.5 percent, the point at which the alcohol kills off the yeast. Sugar is naturally present in the ripe grape. Yeast also occurs naturally as the white bloom on the grape skin. However, this natural yeast is not always used in today's winemaking. Laboratory strains of pure yeast have been isolated and may be used in many situations, each strain contributing something unique to the style of the wine. The carbon dioxide dissipates into the air, except in Champagne and other sparkling wines, in which this gas is retained through a special process.

What are the three major types of wine?

Table wine: approximately 8 to 15 percent alcohol
Sparkling wine: approximately 8 to 12 percent alcohol + CO2
Fortified wine: 17 to 22 percent alcohol

All wine fits into at least one of these categories.

Why do the world's fine wines come only from certain areas?

A combination of factors is at work. The areas with a reputation for fine wines have the right soil and favorable weather conditions, of course. In addition, these areas look at winemaking as an important part of their history and culture.

Is all wine made from the same kind of grape?

No. The major wine grapes come from the species *Vitis vinifera*. In fact, European, North American, Australian, and South American winemakers use the *Vitis vinifera*, which includes many different varieties of grapes—both red and white. However, there are other grapes used for winemaking. The most important native grape species in America is *Vitis labrusca*, which is grown widely in New York State as well as other East Coast and Midwest states. Hybrids, which are also used in modern winemaking, are a cross between *Vitis vinifera* and *Vitis labrusca*.

KEVIN ZRALY'S FAVORITE WINE REGIONS

Napa
Sonoma
Bordeaux
Burgundy
Champagne
Rhône Valley
Tuscany
Piedmont
Mosel
Rhine
Rioja
Douro (Port)
Mendoza
Maipo Valley
South Australia
Stellenbasch

PLANTING OF VINEYARDS for winemaking began more than 8,000 years ago.

A SAMPLING OF THE MAJOR GRAPES

Vitis vinifera
Chardonnay
Cabernet Sauvignon

Vitis labrusca
Concord
Catawba

Hybrids
Seyval Blanc
Baco Noir

VITIS is Latin for vine.
VINUM is Latin for wine.

More than 50 major white wine grape varieties are grown throughout the world.

Other white grapes and regions you may wish to explore:

GRAPES	WHERE THEY GROW BEST
Albariño	Spain
Chenin Blanc	Loire Valley, France; California
Gewürztraminer, Pinot Blanc, Pinot Gris	Alsace, France
Pinot Grigio (aka Pinot Gris)	Italy; California; Oregon
Sémillon	Bordeaux (Sauternes); Australia
Viognier	Rhône Valley, France; California
Grüner Veltliner	Austria

NEW WORLD VS. OLD WORLD

Wines from the United States, Australia, Chile, Argentina, New Zealand, and South Africa usually list the grape variety on the label. French, Italian, and Spanish wines usually list the region, village, or vineyard where the wine was made—but not the grape.

Major White Grapes of the World

ONE OF THE MOST FREQUENTLY ASKED QUESTIONS by my wine students is what will help them most in learning about wine. The main thing is to understand the major grape varieties and where they are grown in the world.

I don't want to overwhelm you with information about every grape under the sun. My job as a wine educator is to try to narrow down this overabundance of data. So let's start off with the three major grapes you need to know to understand white wine. More than 90 percent of all quality white wine is made from these three grapes. They are listed here in order from the lightest style to the fullest:

> Riesling   Sauvignon Blanc   Chardonnay

This is not to say that world-class white wine comes from only these grapes, but knowing these three is a good start.

One of the first things I show my students is a list indicating where these three grape varieties grow best. It looks something like this:

GRAPES	WHERE THEY GROW BEST
Riesling	Germany; Alsace, France; New York State; Washington State
Sauvignon Blanc	Bordeaux, France; Loire Valley, France; New Zealand; California (Fumé Blanc)
Chardonnay	Burgundy, France; Champagne, France; California; Australia

There are world-class Rieslings, Sauvignon Blancs, and Chardonnays made in other countries, but in general the above regions specialize in wines made from these grapes.

COMMON AROMAS

Riesling	*Sauvignon Blanc*	*Chardonnay*
Fruity	Grapefruit	Green apple, Butter, Citrus
Lychee nut	Grass, Herbs	Grapefruit, Melon, Oak
Sweet	Cat pee, Green olive	Pineapple, Toast, Vanilla

Major Red Grapes of the World

AS YOU BEGIN YOUR WINE JOURNEY, you should understand the major red grape varieties and where in the world they produce the best wines.

Let's start with a list of what I consider to be the major red-wine grapes, ranked from lightest to fullest-bodied style, along with the region or country in which the grape grows best. By looking at this chart, not only will you get an idea of the style of the wine, but also a feeling for gradations of weight, color, tannin, and ageability.

THERE ARE hundreds of different red-wine grapes planted throughout the world. California alone grows 31 different red-wine grape varieties.

IN GENERAL, the lighter the color, the more perceived acidity.

TEXTURE	GRAPES	TANNIN LEVEL	WHERE THEY GROW BEST	COLOR LEVEL	AGEABILITY
Light		Low		Lighter	Drink Young
	Gamay		Beaujolais, France		
	Pinot Noir		Burgundy, France; Champagne, France; California; Oregon		
	Tempranillo		Rioja, Spain		
	Sangiovese		Tuscany, Italy		
	Merlot		Bordeaux, France; Napa, California;		
	Zinfandel		California		
	Cabernet Sauvignon		Bordeaux, France; Napa, California; Chile		
	Nebbiolo		Piedmont, Italy		
	Syrah/Shiraz		Rhône Valley, France; Australia; California		
Full-bodied		High		Deeper	Wine to Age

ONCE YOU have become acquainted with these major red-wine grapes, you may wish to explore the following:

GRAPES	WHERE THEY GROW BEST
Barbera	Italy
Dolcetto	Italy
Cabernet Franc	Loire Valley and Bordeaux, France
Grenache/ Garnacha	Rhône Valley, France Spain
Malbec	Bordeaux and Cahors, France; Argentina

To put this chart together is extremely challenging, given all the variables that go into making wine and the many different styles that can be produced. Remember, there are always exceptions to the rule, just as there are other countries and wine regions not listed here that produce world-class wine from some of the red grapes shown. You'll begin to see this for yourself if you do your homework and taste a lot of different wines. Good luck!

NEW WINEMAKING and Grape Growing Catch Words: Reductive winemaking, cold soaking of grapes, phenolic ripening, green harvesting

WINEMAKERS SAY that winemaking begins in the vineyard with the growing of the grapes.

THE MOST important factors in winemaking:
1. Geographic location
2. Soil
3. Weather
4. Grapes
5. Vinification (the actual winemaking process)

VINES ARE planted during their dormant periods, usually in the months of April or May. Most vines will continue to produce good-quality grapes for forty years or more.

DON'T FORGET that the seasons in the Southern Hemisphere—which includes Australia, New Zealand, Chile, Argentina, and South Africa—are reversed.

A VINE doesn't usually produce grapes suitable for winemaking until the third year.

"BRIX" is the winemaker's measure of sugar in grapes.

AS SUGAR levels increase, acidity decreases.

IT TAKES an average of 100 days between a vine's flowering and the harvest.

Does it matter which types of grapes are planted?

Yes, it does. Traditionally, many grape varieties produce better wines when planted in certain locations. For example, most red grapes need a longer growing season than do white grapes, so red grapes are usually planted in warmer locations. In colder northern regions—in Germany and northern France, for instance—most vineyards are planted with white grapes. In the warmer regions of Italy, Spain, and Portugal, and in California's Napa Valley, the red grape thrives.

When is the harvest?

Grapes are picked when they reach the proper sugar/acid/phenolic ratio for the style of wine the vintner wants to produce. Go to a vineyard in June and taste one of the small green grapes. Your mouth will pucker because the grape is so tart and acidic. Return to the same vineyard—even to that same vine—in September or October, and the grapes will taste sweet. All those months of sun have given sugar to the grape as a result of photosynthesis.

June
3% acid
0 Brix

July
2.3% acid
10 Brix

August
1.7% acid
15 Brix

Harvest
September
0.9% acid
22 Brix

What effect does weather have on the grapes?

Weather can interfere with the quality of the harvest, as well as its quantity. In the spring, as vines emerge from dormancy, a sudden frost may stop the flowering, thereby reducing the yields. Even a strong windstorm can affect the grapes adversely at this crucial time. Not enough rain, too much rain, or rain at the wrong time can also wreak havoc.

Rain just before the harvest will swell the grapes with water, diluting the juice and making thin, watery wines. Lack of rain will affect the wines' balance by creating a more powerful and concentrated wine, but will result in a smaller crop. A severe drop in temperature may affect the vines even outside the growing season. Case in point: In New York State the winter of 2003–04 was one of the coldest in fifty years. The result was a major decrease in wine production, with some vineyards losing more than 50 percent of their crop for the 2004 vintage.

Where are the best locations to plant grapes?

Grapes are agricultural products that require specific growing conditions. Just as you wouldn't try to grow oranges in Maine, you wouldn't try to grow grapes at the North Pole. There are limitations on where vines can be grown. Some of these limitations are: the growing season, number of days of sunlight, angle of the sun, average temperature, and rainfall. Soil is of primary concern, and adequate drainage is a requisite. The right amount of sun ripens the grapes properly to give them the sugar/acid balance that makes the difference between fair, good, and great wine.

What can the vineyard owner do in the case of adverse weather?

A number of countermeasures are available to the grower. Some of these measures are used while the grapes are on the vine; others are part of the winemaking process.

PROBLEM	RESULTS IN	SOME SOLUTIONS
Frost	Reduced yield	Various frost protection methods: wind machines, sprinkler systems, and flaming heaters
Not enough sun	Underripe, green herbal, vegetal character, high acid, low sugar	Chaptalization (the addition of sugar to the must—fresh grape juice—during fermentation)

THE TOP countries in vineyard acreage worldwide:
1. Spain
2. France
3. Italy
4. Turkey
5. China
6. United States
7. Iran

SINCE 2001, the largest growth in vineyards has been in China.

"And Noah began to be a husbandman and he planted a vineyard, and he drank of the vine."
GENESIS 9:20–21

- In 2009, major fires hit the Yarra Valley, Australia during the start of the harvest.
- In 2008, a spring frost affected the vineyards all over the state of California. It was the worst frost since the early seventies.
- In 2008, Australia got hit with everything from the worst drought ever and scorching heat in South Australia, and the Hunter Valley had record-breaking rain and major flooding.
- In Alsace, France, a hailstorm in June 2007 destroyed entire vineyards.
- Hailstorms in Mendoza, Argentina, from December 2007 to February 2008 dramatically reduced yields.
- In 2004, Burgundy, suffered major hailstorms in July and August that damaged or destroyed at least 40% of the grapes.
- The historic 2003 heat wave in Europe changed the balance of the traditional style of wines produced in most regions.
- In 2002, the Piedmont region of Italy (Barolo, Barbaresco) was hit with a September hailstorm that destroyed some of the best vineyards in the region.
- Poor weather conditions for the 2002 vintage in Tuscany resulted in no production of Chianti Classico Reserva. Champagne harvest the wettest since 1873.
- From 1989 to 1999 in Bordeaux, France, it rained during the harvest of eight out of ten vintages, which affected picking dates, yields, and the quality of the wine.

PROBLEM	RESULTS IN	SOME SOLUTIONS
Too much sun	Overripe, high alcohol, prune character	Amelioration (addition of water)
Too much rain	Thin, watery wines	Move vineyard to a drier climate
Mildew	Rot	Spray with copper sulfate
Drought	Scorched grapes	Irrigate or pray for rain
High alcohol	Change in the balance of the components	De-alcoholize
High acidity	Sour, tart wine	De-acidify
Phylloxera	Dead vines	Graft vines onto resistant rootstock

What is phylloxera?

Phylloxera, a grape louse, is one of the grapevine's worst enemies, because it eventually kills the entire plant. An epidemic infestation in the 1870s came close to destroying all the vineyards of Europe. Luckily, the roots of native American vines are immune to this louse. After this was discovered, all the European vines were pulled up and grafted onto phylloxera-resistant American rootstocks.

Can white wine be made from red grapes?

Yes. The color of wine comes entirely from the grape skins. By removing the skins immediately after picking, no color is imparted to the wine, and it will be white. In the Champagne region of France, a large percentage of the grapes grown are red, yet most of the resulting wine is white. California's White Zinfandel is made from red Zinfandel grapes.

What is tannin, and is it desirable in wine?

Tannin is a natural substance that comes from the skins, stems, and pips of the grapes, and even from the wooden barrels, such as French oak, in which many wines are aged or fermented. It is a natural preservative; without it, certain wines wouldn't continue to improve in the bottle. A word used to describe the taste sensation of tannin, especially in young wines, is "astringent." Tannin can make the wine taste bitter. But tannin is not a taste. It's a tactile sensation. Generally, red wines have a higher level of tannin than whites, because red grapes are usually left to ferment with their skins. Tannin is also found in strong tea. And what can you add to the tea to make it less astringent? Milk—the fat and the proteins in milk soften the tannin. And so it is with a highly tannic wine. If you take another milk by-product, such as cheese, and have it with wine, it softens the tannin and makes the wine more appealing. Enjoy a beef entrée or one served with a cream sauce and a good bottle of red wine to experience it for yourself.

Is acidity desirable in wine?

All wine will have a certain amount of acidity. Generally, white wines have more perceived acidity than reds, though winemakers try to have a balance of fruit and acid. An overly acidic wine is also described as tart or sour. Acidity is a very important component in the aging of wines.

ONE OF the few countries to escape phylloxera is Chile. Chilean wine producers imported their vines from France in the 1860s, before phylloxera attacked the French vineyards.

IN THE early 1980s, phylloxera became a problem in the vineyards of California. Vineyard owners were forced to replant their vines at a cost of $15,000 to $25,000 per acre, costing the California wine industry over a billion dollars.

WALNUTS AND tea also contain tannin.

BESIDES TANNIN, red wine contains resveratrol, which in medical studies has been associated with anticancer properties.

KING TUTANKHAMEN, who died in 1327 B.C., apparently preferred the taste of red wine, according to scientists who found residues of red wine compounds (tannins) in ancient Egyptian jars found in his tomb.

THE FIRST known reference to a specific vintage was made by Roman scientist Pliny the Elder, who rated the wines of 121 B.C. "of the highest excellence."

2005 WAS a great vintage year in every major wine region on earth!

"The truth of wine aging is that it is unknown, unstudied, poorly understood, and poorly predicted!"
—ZELMA LONG, *California winemaker*

THREE MAJOR wine collectibles that will age more than ten years:
1. Great châteaux of Bordeaux
2. Best producers of California Cabernet Sauvignon
3. Finest producers of vintage Port

What is meant by "vintage"? Why is one year considered better than another?

A vintage indicates the year the grapes were harvested, so every year is a vintage year. A vintage chart reflects the weather conditions for various years. Better weather usually results in a better rating for the vintage, and therefore a higher likelihood that the wine will age well.

Are all wines meant to be aged?

No. It's a common misconception that all wines improve with age. In fact, more than 90 percent of all the wines made in the world should be consumed within one year, and less than 1 percent of the world's wines should be aged for more than five years. Wines change with age. Some get better, but most do not. The good news is that the 1 percent represents more than 350 million bottles of wine every vintage.

What makes a wine last more than five years?

The color and the grape: Red wines, because of their tannin content, will generally age longer than whites. And certain red grapes, such as Cabernet Sauvignon, tend to have more tannin than, say, Pinot Noir.

The vintage: The better the weather conditions in one year, the more likely the wines from that vintage will have a better balance of fruits, acids, and tannins, and therefore have the potential to age longer.

Where the wine comes from: Certain vineyards have optimum conditions for growing grapes, including such factors as soil, weather, drainage, and slope of the land. All of this contributes to producing a great wine that will need time to age.

How the wine was made (vinification): The longer the wine remains in contact with its skins during fermentation (maceration), and if it is fermented and/or aged in oak, the more of the natural preservative tannin it will have, which can help it age longer. These are just two examples of how winemaking can affect the aging of wine.

Wine storage conditions: Even the best-made wines in the world will not age well if they are improperly stored. (See page 55.)

How is wine production regulated worldwide?

Each major wine-producing country has government-sponsored control agencies and laws that regulate all aspects of wine production and set certain minimum standards that must be observed. Here are some examples:

France: Appellation d'Origine Contrôlée (AOC)

Italy: Denominazione di Origine Controllata (DOC)

United States: Alcohol and Tobacco Tax and Trade Bureau

Germany: Ministry of Agriculture

Spain: Denominación de Origen (DO)

5 Bottles of wine produced annually from one grapevine

240 Bottles of wine in a barrel (59 gallons)

720 Bottles of wine from a ton of grapes

5,500 Bottles of wine produced annually from an acre of grapevines

Source: Napa Valley Vintners

A BOTTLE OF wine contains 600-800 grapes (2.4 lbs.).

THERE ARE more than seventy wine-producing countries in the world.

ACCORDING TO *Wines & Vines*, the value of wine sold worldwide is now more than $100 billion.

ON TASTING
WINE

———◆———

THE BASIC AND ADVANCED STEPS OF TASTING WINE

THE PHYSIOLOGY OF WINE SMELLING AND TASTING

THE 60-SECOND WINE EXPERT TASTING METHOD

IF YOU can see through a red wine, it's generally ready to drink!

AS WHITE wines age, they gain color. Red wines, on the other hand, lose color as they age.

ON TASTING WINE

YOU CAN READ all the books (and there are plenty) written on wine to become more knowledge-able on the subject, but the best way to truly enhance your understanding of wine is to taste as many wines as possible. Reading covers the more academic side of wine, while tasting is more enjoyable and practical. A little of each will do you the most good.

The following are the necessary steps for tasting wine. You may wish to follow them with a glass of wine in hand.

Wine tasting can be broken down into five basic steps: Color, Swirl, Smell, Taste, and Savor.

Color

The best way to get an idea of a wine's color is to get a white background—a napkin or table-cloth—and hold the glass of wine on an angle in front of it. The range of colors that you may see depends, of course, on whether you're tasting a white or red wine. Here are the colors for both, beginning with the youngest wine and moving to an older wine:

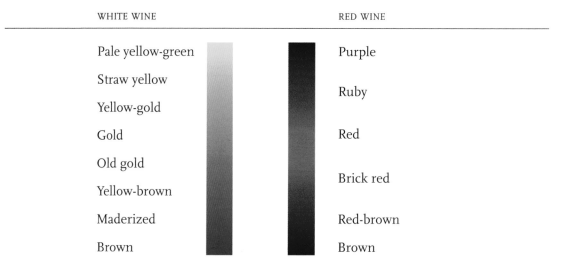

WHITE WINE	RED WINE
Pale yellow-green	Purple
Straw yellow	Ruby
Yellow-gold	
Gold	Red
Old gold	
Yellow-brown	Brick red
Maderized	Red-brown
Brown	Brown

Color tells you a lot about the wine. Since we start with the white wines, let's consider three reasons why a white wine may have more color:

1. It's older.
2. Different grape varieties give different color. (For example, Chardonnay usually gives off a deeper color than does Sauvignon Blanc.)
3. The wine was aged in wood.

When it comes to describing the color of wine, perceptions vary. It's not unusual to hear that some believe that the wine is pale yellow-green, while others say it's gold. There are no right or wrong answers, because perception is subjective. So you can imagine what happens when we actually taste the wine!

Swirl

Why do we swirl wine? To allow oxygen to get into the wine. Swirling releases the esters, ethers, and aldehydes that combine with oxygen to yield a wine's bouquet. In other words, swirling aerates the wine and releases more of the bouquet and aroma.

OXYGEN can be the best friend of a wine, but it can also be its worst enemy. A little oxygen helps release the smell of the wine (as with swirling), but prolonged exposure can be harmful, especially to older wines.

I LIKE to have my students put their hand over the glass of wine when they swirl to create a more powerful bouquet and aroma.

Smell

This is the most important part of wine tasting. You can perceive just four tastes—sweet, sour, bitter, and salty—but the average person can identify more than two thousand different scents, and wine has more than two hundred of its own. Now that you've swirled the wine and released the bouquet, I want you to smell the wine at least three times. You may find that the third smell will give you more information than the first smell did. What does the wine smell like? What type of nose does it have? Smell is the most important step in the tasting process and most people simply don't spend enough time on it.

Pinpointing the nose of the wine helps you to identify certain characteristics. The problem here is that many people in class want me to tell them what the wine smells like. Since I prefer not to use subjective words, I may say that the wine smells like a French white Burgundy. Still, I

BOUQUET IS the total smell of the wine.
Aroma is the smell of the grapes.
"nose" is a word that wine tasters use to describe the bouquet and aroma of the wine.

ONE OF the most difficult challenges in life is to match a smell or a taste with a word that describes it.

Zinfandel	spiciness, blackberry
Cabernet Sauvignon	chocolate, cassis
Old Bordeaux	wet fallen leaves
Old Burgundy	gamey, mushrooms
Rhône	black pepper
Pouilly-Fumé or Sancerre	gunflint
Chablis	mineral
White Burgundy	chalky
Chardonnay	buttery, apple
Sauvignon Blanc	grapefruit
Riesling	green apple
Pinot Noir	red cherry
Gewurztraminer	lychee

WHAT KIND of wine do I like? I like my wine bright, rich, mature, developed, seductive, and with nice legs!

NEED MORE WORDS?

A new book, *Wine Speak*, by Benard Klem, includes 36,975 wine-tasting descriptions. Who knew?

find that this doesn't satisfy the majority of the class. They want to know more. I ask these people to describe what steak and onions smell like. They answer, "Like steak and onions." See what I mean?

The best way to learn what your own preferences are for styles of wine is to "memorize" the smell of the individual grape varieties. For white, just try to memorize the three major grape varieties: Chardonnay, Sauvignon Blanc, and Riesling. Keep smelling them, and smelling them, and smelling them until you can identify the differences, one from the other. For the reds it's a little more difficult, but you still can take three major grape varieties: Pinot Noir, Merlot, and Cabernet Sauvignon. Try to memorize those smells without using flowery words, and you'll understand what I'm talking about.

For those in the Wine School who remain unconvinced, I hand out a list of five hundred different words commonly used to describe wine. Here is a small excerpt:

acetic	character	legs	seductive
aftertaste	corky	light	short
aroma	delicate	maderized	soft
astringent	developed	mature	stalky
austere	earthy	metallic	sulfury
baked-burnt	finish	moldy	tart
balanced	flat	nose	thin
big-full-heavy	fresh	nutty	tired
bitter	grapey	off	vanilla
body	green	oxidized	woody
bouquet	hard	pétillant	yeasty
bright	hot	rich	young

You're also more likely to recognize some of the defects of a wine through your sense of smell. Following is a list of some of the negative smells in wine:

SMELL	WHY
Vinegar	Too much acetic acid in wine
Sherry*	Oxidation
Dank, wet, moldy, cellar smell	Wine absorbs the taste of a defective cork (referred to as "corked wine")
Sulfur (burnt matches)	Too much sulfur dioxide

* Authentic Sherry, from Spain, is intentionally made through controlled oxidation.

All wines contain some sulfur dioxide since it is a by-product of fermentation. Sulfur dioxide is also used in many ways in winemaking. It kills bacteria in wine, prevents unwanted fermentation, and acts as a preservative. It sometimes causes a burning and itching sensation in your nose.

THE PHYSIOLOGY OF WINE SMELLING AND TASTING

One of the most wonderful things about wine is its ability to bring us to our senses. While all of our senses factor into the enjoyment of wine, none does so powerfully or pleasurably as olfaction, our sense of smell combined with our sense of taste.

Happily, most wine tasters regularly experience what evolving scientific understanding also proves: the importance of smell and its impact on everything from learning and loving to aging and health.

How do our sense of smell and taste work, why is smell so emotionally evocative, and why is it so critical to our enjoyment?

EACH PERSON has a different threshold for sulfur dioxide, and although most people do not have an adverse reaction, it can be a problem for individuals with asthma. To protect those who are prone to bad reactions to sulfites, federal law requires winemakers to label their wines with the warning that the wine contains sulfites.

EVERY WINE contains a certain amount of sulfites. They are a natural by-product of fermentation.

THIS JUST in: It is now known that each nostril can detect different smells.

THE OLDEST part of the human brain is the olfactory region.

THE 2004 Nobel Prize for Medicine was awarded to two scientists for their research on the olfactory system and the discovery that there are more than 10,000 different smells!

AS PROOF of the evolutionary importance of smell, 1 to 2 percent of our genes are involved in olfaction, approximately the same percent that is involved in the immune system.

OLFACTORY BULB

LIMBIC SYSTEM

SIZE AND SHAPE do matter. Deep, good wine glasses, such as Riedel's lines of stemware, do much to enhance varietal aroma.

HOW DO WE SMELL?

With each inhalation, the nose gathers essential information about the world around us—its delights, opportunities, and dangers. We can shut our eyes, close our mouths, withdraw our touch, and cover our ears, but the nose, with notable exceptions, is always working, alerting us to potential danger and possible pleasure.

Our sense of smell also enhances learning, evokes memory, promotes healing, cements desire, and inspires us to action. It is so important to the preservation and sustenance of life that the instantaneous information it gathers bypasses the thalamus, where the other senses are processed, and moves directly to the limbic system. The limbic system controls emotions, emotional responses, mood, motivation, and our pain and pleasure sensations, and it is where we analyze olfactory stimuli.

Memory stored in the limbic system uniquely links emotional state with physical sensation, creating our most important and primitive form of learning: working memory. We remember smell differently than we recall sight, sound, taste, or touch because we often respond to smell the same way we respond to emotion: an increased heart rate, enhanced sensitivity, and faster breathing. It is this emotional connection that gives smell the power to stimulate memory so strongly and why a single smell can instantly transport us back to a particular time and place.

In 2004, the Nobel Prize in Medicine was awarded to Columbia University Professor Richard Axel and Hutchinson Cancer Research Center Professor Linda B. Buck for their breakthrough discoveries in olfaction. Axel and Buck discovered a large family of genes in the cells of the epithelium, or lining, of the upper part of the nose that control production of unique protein receptors, called olfactory receptors. Olfactory receptors specialize in recognizing, then attaching themselves to, thousands of specific molecules of incoming odorants. Once attached, the trapped chemical molecules are converted to electrical signals. These signals are relayed to neurons in the olfactory bulbs (there is one in each nasal cavity) before being carried along the olfactory nerve to the primary olfactory cortex, in the brain's limbic system, for analysis and response. By the time the electrical signals of smell are directed to the limbic system, the component parts of a smell—wet leather, wildflowers, golden apples, and river rocks—have already been identified and translated into electric signals. The limbic system recombines these components for analysis by scanning its vast memory data bank for related matches. Once analysis is completed, the limbic

THE OLFACTORY PATHWAY OF PULIGNY-MONTRACHET FROM BOTTLE TO BRAIN

We can trace the olfactory pathway of a Puligny-Montrachet from bottle to brain, through the following steps:
- *We open the bottle, in happy anticipation.*
- *We pour the wine into a proper glass.*
- *We swirl the glass to release the wine's aromas.*
- *We inhale the wine's bouquet deeply and repeatedly.*
- *Chemical components—esters, ethers, aldehydes, etc.—in the wines swirl upward through the nostrils on currents of air.*
- *Midway up the nose, millions of olfactory receptor neurons (olfactory epithelium), with their specialized protein receptors, bind the odorants that form the components of the specific wine profile.*
- *Interaction of the specific odor molecules matched with the right receptor causes the receptor to change shape.*
- *This change gives rise to an electrical signal that goes first to the olfactory bulbs and then to the areas of the brain that convert the electrical signal to the identification of a smell, or group of smells.*
- *The brain associates the smell(s) with perception, impressions, emotions, memories, knowledge, and more.*

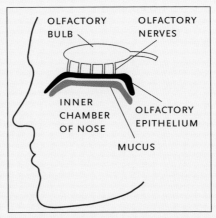

OLFACTORY BULB · OLFACTORY NERVES · INNER CHAMBER OF NOSE · OLFACTORY EPITHELIUM · MUCUS

IMPLICIT MEMORIES are perceptual, emotional, sensory, and are often unconsciously encoded and retrieved. Explicit memories are factual, episodic, temporal, and require conscious coding and retrieval. A good wine, well perceived and described, lives on in both forms of memory.

ALLERGIES, INJURY, illness, and sexual activity are just some of the reasons our noses can become temporarily or permanently clogged or occluded.

system triggers an appropriate physiological response: danger or pleasure, fight or flight. Taste a Puligny-Montrachet, for example, and the limbic system might recognize it as a pleasant white wine made from Chardonnay grapes. More experienced wine tasters, with a more highly developed memory data bank, connect the wine to other Puligny-Montrachets and will recognize it as Puligny. Expert tasters might be able to recall the vineyard, maker, and year. The more we taste, test, and study, the better we become at identification.

Dr. Alan Hirsch of the Smell & Taste Treatment and Research Foundation and experts from the Monell Chemical Senses Center have shed additional light on the evolution and devolution of smell over a lifetime by describing the changes that occur at various periods in the life cycle.

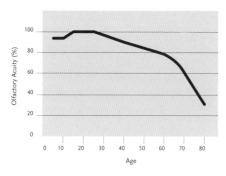

OLFACTORY ACUITY is at its peak in young adulthood.

NUMEROUS STUDIES have proven the power of scents to affect mood and memory. Lavender has the power to calm. Citrus enhances alertness and, as a result, is occasionally broadcast in office buildings in Japan. And, as Shakespeare writes in *Hamlet*, "There's rosemary, that's for remembrance. Pray thee, love, remember."

FIRST IMPRESSIONS? A well-crafted wine's aroma evolves in the glass and our noses quickly become inured to smell. This is why it's advisable to revisit wine's aroma a few times in any given tasting or flight. Tasters can take a cue from the old perfumer's trick of sniffing their sleeves between the many essences/elixirs they may smell on a given day. In other words, they turn to something completely different—balancing sense with non-sense.

Early Childhood: As a child grows, so does his or her ability to recognize and remember different odors, especially those that are paired with an emotional event. At this point in their development, children usually have a hard time describing smells in words, but they are forming lifelong positive and negative sensory and emotional impressions. For example, smelling roses in the garden with Mom will have a far different impact on the feeling the scent elicits later in life than if a child first smells roses at the funeral of a loved one.

Puberty: The sense of smell is at its most acute in both men and women, although women surge further ahead at the onset of menstruation. This heightened sensitivity to smell will persist throughout their fertile years.

Adulthood: Women consistently outscore men in their ability to put names to smells in adulthood, and women give higher ratings on pleasure and intensity, lower ratings on unpleasant aromas. Women's sense of smell is particularly acute at ovulation and during pregnancy.

Midlife: Men and women slowly begin to lose their acuity of smell between the ages of 35 and 40, though the ability to identify and remember smells can continue to improve over the course of a lifetime.

Age 65: By age 65, about half the population will experience a decline of, on average, 33 percent in their olfactory abilities. A quarter of the population has no ability to smell after 65.

Age 80: A majority of the population will show losses of up to 50 percent in olfactory abilities by age 80.

IT'S A GOOD THING WE HAVE TWO!

The septum, made up of cartilage, divides the nose into two separate chambers, or nostrils, each with discreetly wired epithelium and olfactory bulbs. Each nostril serves a different function and operates at peak capacity at different times. It is rare for both nostrils, even in the healthiest noses, to work at full capacity simultaneously, and people with a deviated septum often report being able to breathe out of only one nostril. Jacobson's Organ author Lyall Watson reports, "A three-hour cycle of alternation between left and right nostrils goes on night and day. At night it contributes to sleep movements." Watson hypothesizes that by day, when we are conscious, right and left nostrils direct information to accordant parts of the brain—the right being the side that perceives, intuits, encodes, and stores implicitly; the left being the side that explicitly analyzes, names, records, and retrieves. "Ideally, we need both. . . . But if a situation is strange and requires action based more on prediction than precedent, you would be better off facing it with a clear left nostril."

HOW DO WE TASTE?

Like smell, taste belongs to our chemical sensing system. Taste is detected by special structures called taste buds, and we have, on average, between five thousand and ten thousand of them, mainly on the tongue but with a few at the back of the throat and on the palate. Taste buds are the only sensory cells that are regularly replaced throughout a person's lifetime, with total regeneration taking place approximately every ten days. Scientists are examining this phenomenon, hoping that they will discover ways to replicate the process, inducing regeneration in damaged sensory and nerve cells.

Clustered within each taste bud are gustatory cells that have small gustatory hairs containing gustatory receptors. The gustatory receptors, like the olfactory receptors, are sensitive to specific types of dissolved chemicals. Everything we eat and drink must be dissolved—usually by the saliva—in order for the gustatory receptors to identify its taste. Once dissolved, the gustatory receptors read, then translate, a food's chemical structure before converting that information to electrical signals. These electrical signals are transmitted, via the facial and glossopharyngeal nerves, through the nose and on to the brain where they are decoded and identified as a specific taste.

Our Salivation

Saliva is critical not only to the digestion of food and to the maintenance of oral hygiene, but also to flavor. Saliva dissolves taste stimuli, allowing their chemistry to reach the gustatory receptor cells.

Remember being told to chew your food slowly so that you would enjoy your meal more? It's true. Taking more time to chew food and savor beverages allows more of their chemical components to dissolve and more aromas to be released. This provides more material for the gustatory and olfactory receptors to analyze, sending more complex data to the brain, which enhances perception. Taste and smell intensify.

While the majority of our taste buds are located in the mouth, we also have thousands of additional nerve endings—especially on the moist epithelial surfaces of the mouth, throat, nose, and eyes—that perceive texture, temperature, and assess a variety of factors, which recognize sensations like the prickle of sulfur, the coolness of mint, and the burn of pepper. While humans can

WHAT ARE OUR wine senses? Hearing (as in corks popping, wine pouring), seeing, smelling, tasting, feeling, and reflecting to be sure—but also more. Scientists and experts agree that smell accounts for up to 90% of what many perceive as taste and mouthfeel.

TASTING AND chewing increase the rate of salivary flow.

THERE IS now evidence that people may perceive five tastes: sweet, sour, bitter, salty, and possibly umami—aka MSG.

MUCH OF WHAT is commonly described as taste—80–90% or more—is aroma/bouquet as sensed and articulated by our olfactory receptors, and mouthfeel and texture as sensed by surrounding organs.

OTHER SENSATIONS associated with wine include numbing, tingling, drying, cooling, warming, and coating.

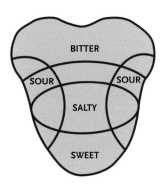

detect an estimated ten thousand smells and smell combinations, we can taste just four tastes—sweet, salty, sour, and bitter. Of these, only sweet, sour, and occasional bitterness are applicable to wine tasting.

Mouthfeel

Mouthfeel is literally how a wine feels in the mouth. These feelings are characterized by sensations that delight, prick, and/or pain our tongue, lips, and cheeks, and that often linger in the mouth after swallowing or spitting. They can range from the piquant tingle of Champagne bubbles to the teeth-tightening astringency of tannin; from the cool expansiveness of menthol/eucalyptus to the heat of a high-alcohol red; and from the cloying sweetness of a low-acid white to the velvet coating of a rich Rhône. The physical feel of wine is important to mouthfeel, and includes: body, thin to full; weight, light to heavy; and texture, austere, unctuous, silky, and chewy. Each contributes to wine's overall balance. More than just impressions, these qualities can trigger physical responses—drying, puckering, and salivation—which can literally have wines dancing on the tongue and clinging to the teeth.

What should you think about when tasting wine?

Be aware of the most important sensations of taste and your own personal thresholds to those tastes. Also, pay attention to where they occur on your tongue and in your mouth. As I mentioned earlier, you can perceive just four tastes: sweet, sour, bitter, and salty (but there's no salt in wine, so we're down to three). Bitterness in wine is usually created by high alcohol and high tannin. Sweetness occurs only in wines that have some residual sugar left over after fermentation. Sour (sometimes called "tart") indicates the acidity in wine.

    Sweetness: The highest threshold is on the tip of the tongue. If there's any sweetness in a wine whatsoever, you'll get it right away.

    Acidity: Found at the sides of the tongue, the cheek area, and the back of the throat. White wines and some lighter-style red wines usually contain a higher degree of acidity.

Bitterness: Tasted on the back of the tongue.

Tannin: The sensation of tannin begins in the middle of the tongue. Tannin frequently exists in red wines or white wines aged in wood. When the wines are too young, tannin dries the palate to excess. If there's a lot of tannin in the wine, it can actually coat your whole mouth, blocking the fruit. Remember, tannin is not a taste: It is a tactile sensation.

Fruit and varietal characteristics: These are not tastes, but smells. The weight of the fruit (the "body") will be felt in the middle of the tongue.

Aftertaste: The overall taste and balance of the components of the wine that lingers in your mouth. How long does the balance last? Usually a sign of a high-quality wine is a long, pleasing aftertaste. The taste of many of the great wines lasts anywhere from one to three minutes, with all their components in harmony.

SMELL AND TASTE TOGETHER

Recent research presents proof that taste seldom works alone (something wine tasters have known for centuries) and provides clear scientific evidence that olfaction is uniquely "dual." We often smell by inhaling through nose and mouth simultaneously, adding to smell's complexity.

There are two paths by which smells can reach the olfactory receptors:

Orthonasal stimulation: Odor compounds (smells) reach the olfactory bulb via the "external nares" or nostrils.

Retronasal stimulation: Odor compounds reach the olfactory bulb via the "internal nares," located inside the mouth (the respiratory tract at the back of the throat). This is why even if you pinch your nose shut, a strong cheese inhaled through the mouth may still smell. Molecules that stimulate the olfactory receptors float around in your mouth, up through your internal nares, and stimulate the olfactory neurons in the olfactory bulb.

According to an article in a recent issue of the journal *Neuron,* researchers reported that the smell of chocolate stimulated different brain regions when introduced into the olfactory system through the nose (orthonasally) than it did when introduced through the mouth (retronasally). The study suggests that sensing odor through the nose may help indicate the availability of food while identification through the mouth may signify receipt of food.

TASTING WINE is confirming what the color and smell are telling you.

TANNIN: Think gritty.
BITTER: Think endive or arugula.

DAYTIME DRINKING

No scientific evidence shows that our olfactory abilities change over the course of a day, although many winemakers and wine professionals believe their senses to be keener and their palates cleaner in the morning. When evaluating wines for my wine class and books, I prefer to taste around 11 a.m. Others prefer tasting wine with a slight edge of hunger, which seems to enhance their alertness. Get to know your own cycles!

Super-tasters can be supersensitive, and they may find wines with tannin and high alcohol too bitter; so Cabernet Sauvignon, for example, may not be to their liking. They may also be put off by any sweetness in wine. Non-tasters are the opposite; they might not be bothered by tannin or high alcohol, and sweet wines would probably be perfectly acceptable.

35% OF WOMEN and 15% of men are super-tasters.

THE AVERAGE person has 5,000 taste buds (That means that some of you have 10,000 and some of you have more!).

SUPER-TASTERS have more than 10,000 taste buds.

The overall word for what we perceive in food and drink through a combination of smelling, tasting, and feeling is flavor, with smell being so predominant of the three that I often say that wine tasting is actually "wine smelling," and some chemists describe wine as "a tasteless liquid that is deeply fragrant." It is flavor that lets us know whether we are eating an apple or a pear, drinking a Puligny-Montrachet or an American Chardonnay. Anyone doubting the importance of smell in determining taste is encouraged to hold his or her nose while eating chocolate or cheese, either of which will tend to taste like chalk.

WHO ARE YOU?

According to Janet Zimmerman, writing in Science of the Kitchen: Taste and Texture, *approximately one quarter of the population are "super-tasters," one quarter are "non-tasters," and the remaining half are "tasters." Super-tasters have a significantly higher number of taste buds than tasters, and both groups outnumber non-tasters for taste buds. The averages for the three groups are 96 taste buds per square centimeter for non-tasters, 184 for tasters, and a whopping 425 for super-tasters. Super-tasters tend to taste everything more intensely. Sweets are sweeter, bitters are bitterer, and many foods and beverages, including alcohol, taste and feel unpleasantly strong. Non-tasters are far from picky, and seem less conscious of and therefore less engaged with what they eat and drink. Tasters, the largest and least homogeneous group, vary in their personal preferences but tend to enjoy the widest array of food and drink and relish the act of eating and drinking the most of the three groups.*

TOWARD A COMMON LANGUAGE OF TASTE AND SMELL

Smell is a relatively inadequate word for our most primitive and powerful sense. It means both the smells that emanate from us (we are what we eat and drink) as well as the smells we perceive. Throughout history, wine tasters have done much to create a common language, and to savor the intersection where enlivened and articulated senses meet memory, anticipation, association, and personal preferences throughout history.

Like colors, aroma can be broken down into basic categories which, when combined, yield the rich symphony that is wine. The University of California, Davis's Wine Aroma Wheel, created by

Ann Nobel, categorizes basic fruit aromas as citrus (grapefruit, lemon), berry (blackberry, raspberry, strawberry, black currant), tree (cherry, apricot, peach, apple), tropical (pineapple, melon, banana), dried (raisin, prune, fig), and others. Likewise, vegetative aromas can be categorized as fresh (stemmy, grassy, green, eucalyptus, mint), canned (asparagus, olive, artichoke), and dried (hay, straw, tea, tobacco). Other aroma categories include nutty, caramelized, woody, earthy, chemical, pungent, floral, and spicy.

Still, no two people are alike in either how they smell and taste or what smells and tastes they experience. It is deeply personal and experiential. So, here's to your health and happiness, and to savoring wine and life in and with every sense!

Savor

After you've had a chance to taste the wine, sit back for a few moments and savor it. Think about what you just experienced, and ask yourself the following questions to help focus your impressions:

- Was the wine light, medium, or full-bodied?
- For a white wine: How was the acidity? Very little, just right, or too much?
- For a red wine: Is the tannin in the wine too strong or astringent? Does it blend with the fruit or overpower it?
- What is the strongest component (residual sugar, fruit, acid, tannin)?
- How long did the balance of the components last (ten seconds, sixty seconds, etc.)?
- Is the wine ready to drink? Or does it need more time to age? Or is it past its prime?
- What kind of food would you enjoy with the wine?
- To your taste, is the wine worth the price?
- This brings us to the most important point. The first thing you should consider after you've tasted a wine is whether or not you like it. Is it your style?

You can compare tasting wine to browsing in an art gallery. You wander from room to room looking at the paintings. Your first impression tells whether or not you like something. Once you decide you like a piece of art, you want to know more: Who was the artist? What is the history behind

---

LANGUAGE OF TASTE AND SMELL

Finding the language to describe what we taste and smell, and how what we taste and smell affects us, evolves over our lifetime, with women being slightly better at it than men.

DIFFERENT TASTES AND SMELLS OF WINE COME FROM:

The grape
The winemaking
The aging

WINE TEXTURES:
Light—skim milk
Medium—whole milk
Full—heavy cream

"The key to great wine is balance, and it is the sum of the different parts that make a wine not only delicious but complete and fascinating as well as worthy of aging."
—FIONA MORRISON, M.W.

"A wine goes in my mouth, and I just see it. I see it in three dimensions. The textures. The flavors. The smells. They just jump out at me. I can taste with a hundred screaming kids in a room. When I put my nose in a glass, it's like tunnel vision. I move into another world, where everything around me is just gone, and every bit of mental energy is focused on that wine."
—ROBERT M. PARKER JR., *author and wine critic, in* The Atlantic Monthly

Varietal character
Balance of components
Complexity
Sense of place
Emotional response

SOME FACTORS that contribute to the making of a bad wine are:
- Faulty corks
- Poor selection of grapes
- Bad weather
- Bad winemaking
- High alcohol and tannin (bitterness)
- Herbaceousness
- Bacteria and yeast problems
- Unwanted fermentation in the bottle
- Hydrogen sulfide (rotten-egg smell)
- Excess sulfur dioxide
- Poor winery hygiene
- Unclean barrels
- Poor storage

"Great wine is about nuance, surprise, subtlety, expression, qualities that keep you coming back for another taste. Rejecting a wine because it is not big enough is like rejecting a book because it is not long enough, or a piece of music because it is not loud enough."
—KERMIT LYNCH, Adventures on the Wine Route

Step One: Look at the color of the wine.
Step Two: Smell the wine three times.
Step Three: Put the wine in your mouth and leave it there for three to five seconds.
Step Four: Swallow the wine.
Step Five: Wait and concentrate on the wine for 60 seconds before discussing it.

the work? How was it done? And so it is with wine. Usually, once oenophiles (wine aficionados) discover a wine that they like, they want to learn everything about it: the winemaker; the grapes; exactly where the vines were planted; the blend, if any; and the history behind the wine.

How do you know if a wine is good or not?

The definition of a good wine is one that you enjoy. I cannot emphasize this enough. Trust your own palate and do not let others dictate taste to you!

When is a wine ready to drink?

This is one of the most frequently asked questions in my Wine School. The answer is very simple: when all components of the wine are in balance to your individual taste.

The 60-Second Wine Expert Tasting Method

Over the last few years I have insisted that my students spend one minute in silence after they swallow the wine. For my students to record their impressions, I use a "60-second wine expert" tasting sheet similar to the tasting notes included in this journal. The minute is divided into four sections: 0 to 15 seconds, 15 to 30 seconds, 30 to 45 seconds, and the final 45 to 60 seconds. Try this with your next glass of wine.

Please note that the first taste of wine is a shock to your taste buds. This is due to the alcohol content, acidity, and sometimes the tannin in the wine. The higher the alcohol or acidity, the more of a shock. For the first wine in any tasting, it is probably best to take a sip and swirl it around in your mouth, but don't evaluate it. Wait another thirty seconds, try it again, and then begin the 60-second wine expert.

0 to 15 seconds: If there is any residual sugar/sweetness in the wine, I will experience it now. If there is no sweetness in the wine, the acidity is usually at its strongest sensation in the first fifteen seconds. I am also looking for the fruit level of the wine and its balance with the acidity or sweetness.

15 to 30 seconds: After the sweetness or acidity, I am looking for great fruit sensation. After all, that is what I am paying for! By the time I reach thirty seconds, I am hoping for balance of all the components. By this time, I can identify the weight of the wine. Is it light, medium, or full-bodied? I am now starting to think about what kind of food I can pair with this wine.

30 to 45 seconds: At this point I am beginning to formulate my opinion of the wine, whether I like it or not. Not all wines need sixty seconds of thought. Lighter-style wines, such as Rieslings, will usually show their best at this point. The fruit, acid, and sweetness of a great German Riesling should be in perfect harmony from this point on. For quality red and white wines, acidity—which is a very strong component (especially in the first thirty seconds)—should now be in balance with the fruit of the wine.

45 to 60 seconds: Very often wine writers use the term "length" to describe how long the components, balance, and flavor continue in the mouth. I concentrate on the length of the wine in these last fifteen seconds. In big, full-bodied red wines from Bordeaux and the Rhône Valley, Cabernets from California, Barolos and Barbarescos from Italy, and even some full-bodied Chardonnays, I am concentrating on the level of tannin in the wine. Just as the acidity and fruit balance are my major concerns in the first thirty seconds, it is now the tannin and fruit balance I am looking for in the last thirty seconds. If the fruit, tannin, and acid are all in balance at sixty seconds, then I feel that the wine is probably ready to drink. Does the tannin overpower the fruit? If it does at the sixty-second mark, I will then begin to question whether I should drink the wine now or put it away for more aging.

It is extremely important to me that if you want to learn the true taste of the wine, you take at least one minute to concentrate on all of its components. In my classes it is amazing to see more than a hundred students silently taking one minute to analyze a wine. Some close their eyes, some bow their heads in deep thought, others write notes.

One final point: Sixty seconds to me is the minimum time to wait before making a decision about a wine. Many great wines continue to show balance well past 120 seconds. The best wine I ever tasted lasted more than three minutes—that's three minutes of perfect balance of all components!

THE CELEBRATION OF WINE AND LIFE: THE TOAST

To complete the five senses (sight, hearing, smell, taste, and touch), don't forget to toast your family and friends with the clinking of the glasses. This tradition started in ancient times when the Greeks, afraid of being poisoned by their enemies, shared a little of their wine with one another. If someone had added something to the wine, it would be a short evening for everyone! The clinking of the glasses also is said to drive away the "bad spirits" that might exist and cause the next-day hangover!

I WILL make my decision about whether or not I like the style of a wine within 45 to 60 seconds.

FREQUENTLY ASKED
QUESTIONS
ABOUT WINE

FREQUENTLY ASKED QUESTIONS ABOUT WINE

What happens when I can't finish the whole bottle of wine?

THIS IS ONE OF THE MOST frequently asked questions. If you still have a portion of the wine left over, whether it be red or white, the bottle should be corked and immediately put into the refrigerator. Don't leave it out on your kitchen counter. Remember, bacteria grow in warm temperatures, and a 70°F+ kitchen will spoil wine very quickly. By refrigerating the wine, most wines will not lose their flavor over a forty-eight-hour period. (Some people swear that the wine even tastes better.)

Eventually, the wine will begin to oxidize. This is true of all table wines with an 8 to 14 percent alcohol content. Other wines, such as Ports and Sherries, with a higher alcohol content of 17 to 21 percent, will last longer, but I wouldn't suggest keeping them longer than two weeks.

Another way of preserving wine for an even longer period of time is to buy a small decanter that has a corked top and fill the decanter to the top with the wine. Or go to a hobby or craft store that also carries home winemaking equipment and buy some half bottles and corks.

Remember, the most harmful thing to wine is oxygen, and the less contact with oxygen, the longer the wine will last. That's why some wine collectors also use something called the Vacu-Vin, which pumps air out of the bottle. Other wine collectors spray the bottle with an inert gas such as nitrogen, which is odorless and tasteless, that preserves the wine from oxygen.

If all else fails, you'll still have a great cooking wine!

Do all wines need corks?

It is a time-honored tradition more than two centuries old to use corks to preserve wine. Most corks come from cork oak trees grown in Portugal and Spain.

The fact is that most wines could be sold without using cork as a stopper. Since 90 percent of all wine is meant to be consumed within one year, a screw cap will work just as well, if not better, than a cork for most wines.

Just think what this would mean to you—no need for a corkscrew, no broken corks, and, most important, no more tainted wine caused by contaminated cork.

I do believe that certain wines—those with potential to age for more than five years—are probably better off using cork. But also keep in mind, for those real wine collectors, that a cork's life span is approximately twenty-five to thirty years, after which you'd better drink the wine or find somebody to recork it.

Some wineries now use a synthetic cork made from high-grade thermoplastic that is FDA-approved and also recyclable. These corks form a near-perfect seal, so leakage, evaporation, and off flavors are virtually eliminated. They open with traditional corkscrews and allow wine to be stored upright.

But many wineries around the world use the Stelvin Screw Cap, especially in California (Bonny Doon, Sonoma Cutrer, etc.), Australia, New Zealand, and Austria.

NINETY-THREE PERCENT of New Zealand's bottles have screw-caps, as does seventy-five percent of Australia's.

What is a "corked" wine?

This is a very serious problem for wine lovers! There are some estimates that 3 to 5 percent of all wines have been contaminated and spoiled by a faulty cork. The principal cause of corked wine is a compound called TCA, short for 2,4,6-trichloranisole.

When we find such a bottle at the Wine School, we make sure that every student gets a chance to smell a "corked" wine. It's a smell they won't soon forget!

Some of my students describe it as a dank, wet, moldy, cellar smell, and some describe it as a wet cardboard smell. It overpowers the fruit smell in the wine, making the wine undrinkable. It can happen in a ten-dollar bottle of wine or a thousand-dollar bottle of wine.

What's that funny-looking stuff attached to the bottom of my cork?

ACIDS FOUND in wine:
1. Tartaric
2. Malic
3. Citric

Tartaric acid, or tartrates, is sometimes found on the bottom of a bottle of wine or the cork. Tartaric acid is a harmless crystalline deposit that looks like glass or rock candy. In red wines, the crystals take on a rusty, reddish-brown color from the tannin.

Most tartrates are removed at the winery by lowering the temperature of the wine before it is bottled. Obviously this does not work with all wines, and if you keep your wine at a very cold temperature for a long period of time (for example, in your refrigerator), you can end up with this deposit on your cork.

Cool-climate regions like Germany have a greater chance of producing the crystallization effect.

Does the age of the vine affect the quality of the wine?

You will sometimes see on French wine labels the term Vieilles Vignes ("old vines"). In California, I've tasted many Zinfandels that were made from vines that were more than seventy-five years old. In many wine regions around the world, they are still producing wine made from over one-hundred year old vines. Many wine tasters, including myself, believe that these old vines create a different complexity and taste than do younger vines.

In many countries, grapes from vines three years old or younger cannot be made into a winery's top wine. In Bordeaux, France, Château Lafite-Rothschild produces a second wine, called Carruades de Lafite-Rothschild, which is made from the vineyard's youngest vines (less than fifteen years old).

As a vine gets older, especially over thirty years, it starts losing its fruit-production value. In commercial vineyards, vines will slow down their production at about twenty years of age, and most vines are replanted by their fiftieth birthday.

What is the best wine to age?

THE GREAT CHÂTEAUX OF BORDEAUX

Many great wine regions on Earth produce red wines that will age for thirty or more years. But nowhere on Earth is there a region that produces both red and white wines that you can drink 100 years later!

What is the best bottle size for aging?

MAGNUM (1.5 LITERS)

This is not just my opinion—my friends who collect and make wine all say that their best wines will last longer and mature more slowly in a magnum (the equivalent of two bottles) than in a 750 ml.

One of the theories for this difference in bottle-size aging is the amount of air that is in the bottle (the air between the wine and the cork) versus the quantity of wine.

It's also more fun to serve a magnum at a dinner party.

What are the best wine regions for a vacation?

A great vacation for me is great wine, fabulous restaurants, perfect climate, proximity to the ocean, beautiful scenery (am I asking too much yet?), and nice people! These three wine regions fulfill all my needs:

NAPA VALLEY, CALIFORNIA
TUSCANY, ITALY
BORDEAUX, FRANCE

BOTTLE SIZES

375 ml = 12.7 oz = half-bottle
750 ml = 24.4 oz = full bottle
1.5 liters = 50.8 oz = magnum (bottles)
3 liters = 101.6 oz = double magnum (4 bottles)
6 liters = 203.2 oz = Imperial (8 bottles)
9 liters = 304.8 oz = Salmanazar (12 bottles)

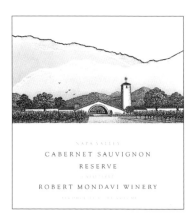

WHICH WINE REGIONS IN THE WORLD PRODUCE THE BEST WINES?

What are the best places for Cabernet Sauvignon?

BORDEAUX, FRANCE (MÉDOC)
RUNNER-UP—CALIFORNIA

In my opinion the best wines of the world are the Great Châteaux of Bordeaux. The primary grape of the Médoc wine is Cabernet Sauvignon. These are not only the best wines for investment, they are some of the best wines to age. With thousands of Châteaux, there's plenty of wine to choose from at all different price points.

What are the best places for Pinot Noir?

BURGUNDY, FRANCE
RUNNERS-UP—OREGON AND CALIFORNIA

Burgundy is a region deep in history and tradition. Vines have been planted there for over a thousand years, and the sensuous Pinot Noir is the only red grape allowed (other than Beaujolais).

The only problems with a great Pinot Noir from Burgundy are its price tag and availability.

What are the best places for Riesling?

GERMANY
RUNNER-UP—ALSACE, FRANCE

Many professionals and wine connoisseurs believe that the best white wine made in the world is Riesling. It is definitely one of the best wines to go with food, especially with lighter-style fish dishes, such as sole and flounder.

I still think that the consumer is confused by the Riesling grape variety and thinks that all Rieslings are sweet. The reality is that 90 percent of all Alsace Rieslings are dry, and most of the German Rieslings I would classify as off-dry or semisweet.

Even though I probably drink more Alsace Rieslings than German Rieslings, the diversity of style of the German wines—dry, off-dry, semisweet, and very sweet—is the reason I would rank German Rieslings as the best in the world.

What are the best places for Sauvignon Blanc?

LOIRE VALLEY, FRANCE
RUNNER-UP—NEW ZEALAND
The Sauvignon Blanc produced in the Loire Valley is best known by its regional names, Sancerre and Pouilly-Fumé. The best of the New Zealand Sauvignon Blancs are sold under the producer's name.

The stylistic differences between the Sauvignon Blancs of the Loire Valley and New Zealand are striking. While both Sauvignon Blancs are medium in body with high acidity, and while both work well with fish and poultry, the New Zealand Sauvignon Blancs have what some would call a very aggressive tropical citrus bouquet that you either like or don't like, which continues in the taste. I like it!

What are the best places for Chardonnay?

BURGUNDY, FRANCE
RUNNER-UP—CALIFORNIA
As much as I like the best producers of California Chardonnay, the elegance and balance of fruit, acidity, alcohol, and oak in a white Burgundy wine are unmatched in the world. From the non-oak-aged Chablis to the barrel-fermented and barrel-aged Montrachets, to the light, easy-drinking Mâcons and the world-famous Pouilly-Fuissé, there is a style and price for everyone.

What are the best places for Merlot?

BORDEAUX, FRANCE (ST-ÉMILION, POMEROL)
RUNNER-UP—CALIFORNIA
The great châteaux of St-Émilion and Pomerol both produce wines made primarily of the Merlot grape. The major difference between the two is the price and availability. St-Émilion is a much larger region than Pomerol, with many more châteaux, offering a better price/value relationship than Pomerol. So for my money I'd go with St-Émilion, based on its lower price and also because today it is the most progressive of all the Bordeaux wine regions.

What is the best after-dinner wine?

PORT
You don't need to drink a lot of Port to get the full enjoyment. One glass of this sweet and fortified (20 percent alcohol) wine ends a meal with a satisfying taste.

Most of the Port that I consume—whether it be Ruby, Tawny, or Vintage—I drink between September and March, the cooler months in the Northeast. For me, the best way to enjoy Port is when it's twenty degrees (or colder) and snowing outside—after the kitchen and all the dishes have been cleaned, your children are tucked away into their dream world, and you are sitting in front of your fireplace with your golden retriever by your side!

Beaux Frères
2005 Pinot Noir
Willamette Valley
Unfined and Unfiltered
ALC. 14.2% BY VOL

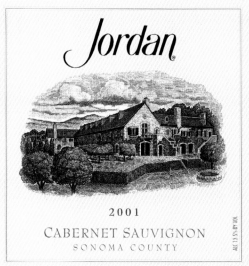

Jordan

2001

CABERNET SAUVIGNON
SONOMA COUNTY

ALC 13.5% BY VOL

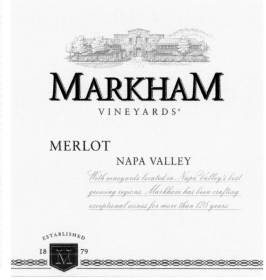

MARKHAM
VINEYARDS®

MERLOT
NAPA VALLEY

With vineyards located in Napa Valley's best
growing regions, Markham has been crafting
exceptional wines for more than 125 years.

ESTABLISHED
18   79

CLOUDY BAY

PINOT NOIR 2007

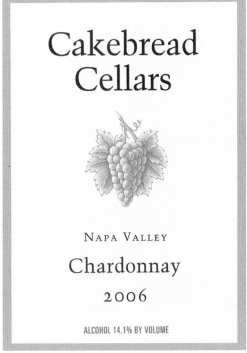

Cakebread
Cellars

Napa Valley

Chardonnay

2006

ALCOHOL 14.1% BY VOLUME

ALSACE   FRANCE
APPELLATION ALSACE CONTRÔLÉE

DEPUIS   1626

TRIMBACH
MARQUE DÉPOSÉE

RIESLING

12.5% alc./vol.   750 ml
MIS EN BOUTEILLES PAR F.E. TRIMBACH A RIBEAUVILLE - ALSACE - FRANCE
PRODUCT OF FRANCE   CONTIENT DES SULFITES   PRODUIT DE FRANCE

WINE-BUYING STRATEGIES

WINE-BUYING STRATEGIES FOR YOUR WINE CELLAR

VINTAGE BEST BETS

TOP VALUE WINE REGIONS

Rías Baixas (Spain)
Mendoza (Argentina)
Marlborough (New Zealand)
Chianti (Italy)
Côtes du Rhône (France)
Maipo (Chile)

WHAT KIND OF WINE BUYER ARE YOU?

"Enthusiast"
"Image Seeker"
"Savvy Shopper"
"Traditionalist"
"Satisfied Sipper"
"Overwhelmed"

—FROM CONSTELLATION WINES U.S.

WINE-BUYING STRATEGIES FOR YOUR WINE CELLAR

BUYING AND SELECTING WINES FOR YOUR CELLAR is the most fun and interesting part of wine appreciation—besides drinking it, of course! You've done all your studying and reading on the wines you like, and now you go out to your favorite wine store to banter with the owner or wine manager. You already have an idea what you can spend and how many bottles you can safely store until they're paired with your favorite foods and friends.

Wine buying has changed dramatically over the last twenty years. Many liquor stores have become wine-specialty stores, and both the consumer and retailer are much more knowledgeable. Even twenty years ago, the wines of South Africa, Spain, New Zealand, Australia, Chile, and Argentina were not the wines the consumer cared to buy. Back then, the major players were the wines of California, France, and Italy. Today there's so much more diversity in wine styles and wine prices, it's almost impossible to keep up with every new wine and new vintage that comes on the market. You can subscribe, among many publications, to *Wine Spectator*, *The Wine Enthusiast*, *Wine & Spirits*, or *Wine Advocate*, Robert M. Parker Jr.'s newsletter, to help you with your choices, but ultimately you'll find the style of wine to suit your own personal taste.

I don't recommend specific wines from specific years because I don't believe that everyone will enjoy the same wines, or that everyone has the same taste buds as I do. I think it's very important that every year the consumers have a general knowledge of wineries that have consistently made great value wine, and know what's hot and what's not. Here are some of my thoughts and strategies for buying wine this year.

There is, and will continue to be, an abundance of fine wine over the next few years. The vintage years of 2000, 2003, and 2005 in Bordeaux; 2001, 2004, 2005, and 2006 in Piedmont and Tuscany; 2003, 2004, 2005, and 2006 in Germany; 2003, 2005, and 2006 in the Rhône Valley; 2002, 2003, and 2005 in Burgundy reds; 2005 and 2007 in Chile, 2006 and 2008 in Argentina; and 2004, 2005, and 2008 in Australian Shiraz will give us great wines to drink over the next few years. The 2002, 2005, 2006, and 2007 vintages for California Cabernet Sauvignon, and 2005 and 2007 Chardonnays are generally excellent. The 1994, 2000, and 2003 vintage Ports are readily available. Although many of the wines from these regions are high-priced, there still remain hundreds of wines under twenty dollars that you can drink now or cellar for the future.

Anyone can buy expensive wines! In an average year I taste some three thousand wines. This past year I tasted over 6,000 wines! The real challenge is finding the best values—the ten-dollar bottle that tastes like a twenty-dollar bottle. The following is a list of my buying strategies for my own wine cellar. This is by no means a complete roster of great wines, but most are retasted every year and have been consistently good.

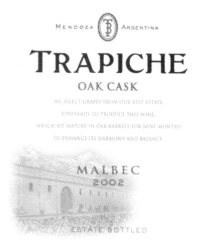

EVERYDAY WINES
($10 and under)

Argentina

Alamos Malbec and Bonarda
Bodega Norton Malbec
Bodegas Esmeralda Malbec
Trapiche Malbec
Valentin Bianchi Malbec

Australia

Alice White Cabernet Sauvignon
Banrock Station Chardonnay and Shiraz
Black Opal Cabernet Sauvignon and Shiraz
Bogle Sauvignon Blanc
Jacob's Creek Shiraz/Cabernet
Lindemans Shiraz Bin 50 or Cabernet
    Sauvignon Bin 45 or Chardonnay Bin 65
Oxford Landing Sauvignon Blanc
Yellow Tail

California

Beaulieu Coastal Merlot and Sauvignon Blanc
Beringer Founders' Estate Cabernet Sauvignon
Buena Vista Sauvignon Blanc
Cline Syrah and Zinfandel

Fetzer Valley Oaks Merlot
Forest Glen Cabernet Sauvignon or Shiraz
    or Merlot
Forest Ville Cabernet Sauvignon or
    Chardonnay
Glass Mountain Cabernet Sauvignon
Kendall Jackson Vintner's Reserve Sauvignon
    Blanc
Kenwood Sauvignon Blanc
McManis Cabernet Sauvignon
Monterey Vineyard Cabernet Sauvignon
Napa Ridge Merlot
Pepperwood Grove Chardonnay
Rutherford Ranch Chardonnay
Smoking Loon Syrah

Chile

Caliterra Cabernet Sauvignon or Merlot
Carmen Carménère
Montes Cabernet Sauvignon
Santa Rita 120 Cabernet Sauvignon
Veramonte Sauvignon Blanc
Walnut Crest Merlot

France

Fortant de France Merlot or Syrah
Guigal Côtes du Rhône
J. Vidal-Fleury Côtes du Rhône
Jaboulet Côtes du Rhône Parallele "45"
La Vieille Ferme Côtes du Ventoux
Louis Latour Ardèche Chardonnay
Louis Jadot or Georges Duboeuf
    Beaujolais-Villages
Mâcon-Villages (most producers)
Michel Lynch
Perrin & Fils Côtes du Rhône
Réserve St-Martin Merlot

Italy

Casal Thaulero Montepulciano Red
Michele Chiarlo Barbera d'Asti

Portugal

Aveleda Vinho Verde

South Africa

Jardin Syrah
Goats do Roam

Washington State

Columbia Crest Sémillon-Chardonnay
Covey Run Fumé Blanc
Hogue Columbia Valley Chardonnay
Hogue Fumé Blanc

ONCE-A-WEEK WINES
($10 to $20)

Argentina

Alamos Chardonnay
Bodegas Catena Zapata
Bodegas Weinert Carrascal
Catena Zapata Cabernet Sauvignon
Clos de los Siete Vista Flores
Domaine Jean Bousquet Malbec
Finca Flichman Gestos Malbec
Kaiken Cabernet Sauvignon Ultra
Navarro Correas Cabernet Sauvignon
    "Collection Privada"
Salentein Malbec Gruro Reserva

Australia

Greg Norman Estate Shiraz
McWilliams Shiraz
Penfolds Shiraz Bin 28
Peter Lehmann Barossa Shiraz
Rosemount Estate Chardonnay or Shiraz/
    Cabernet (Diamond Label)
Rosemount Show Reserve Chardonnay
Wolf Blass Chardonnay

California

Benziger Chardonnay, Merlot, or Cabernet Sauvignon

Bogle Zinfandel

Brander Sauvignon Blanc

Calera Central Coast Chardonnay

Carmenet Cabernet Sauvignon

Castle Rock Pinot Noir

Chateau St. Jean Chardonnay or Sauvignon Blanc

Cline Cellars Zinfandel

Clos du Bois Chardonnay, Merlot, and Syrah

Estancia Chardonnay or Cabernet Sauvignon

Ferrari-Carano Fumé Blanc

Fetzer Valley Oaks Cabernet Sauvignon, Zinfandel, or Chardonnay

Francis Ford Coppola Rosso

Frei Brothers Merlot

Frog's Leap Sauvignon Blanc

Gallo of Sonoma Chardonnay, Cabernet Sauvignon, Pinot Noir, and Merlot

Geyser Peak Sauvignon Blanc

Girard Sauvignon Blanc

Hawk Crest Chardonnay, Cabernet Sauvignon, or Merlot

Hess Select Chardonnay or Cabernet Sauvignon

Honig Sauvignon Blanc

Kendall-Jackson Chardonnay Vintners Reserve, Syrah, or Cabernet Sauvignon

Laurel Glen Quintana Cabernet Sauvignon

Liberty School Cabernet Sauvignon

Markham Merlot and Sauvignon Blanc

Mason Sauvignon Blanc

Meridian Chardonnay or Cabernet Sauvignon

Merryvale Starmont Chardonnay

Ridge Sonoma Zinfandel

Robert Mondavi Private Selection

Rutherford Vintners Cabernet Sauvignon or Merlot

Saintsbury Chardonnay

Sebastiani Chardonnay or Cabernet Sauvignon

Seghesio Sonoma Zinfandel

Silverado Sauvignon Blanc

Simi Cabernet Sauvignon or Sauvignon Blanc or Chardonnay

Souverain Chardonnay and Merlot

St. Francis Merlot or Old Vines Zinfandel

St. Supery Sauvignon Blanc

Trefethen Eshcol Cabernet and Chardonnay

Chile

Casa Lapostolle Cabernet Sauvignon or Merlot Cuvée Alexandre

Concha y Toro Casillero del Diablo or Puente Alto Cabernet Sauvignon

Cousiño-Macul Antiguas Reserva Cabernet Sauvignon

Los Vascos Reserve Cabernet Sauvignon

Montes Merlot

Santa Rita Cabernet Sauvignon or Casa Real Sauvignon Blanc

Veramonte Primus

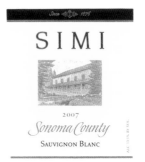

France

Château Bonnet Blanc

Château Greysac

Château La Cardonne

Château Larose-Trintaudon

Drouhin Vero Chardonnay or Pinot Noir

Georges Duboeuf Fleurie

Georges Duboeuf Pouilly-Fuissé

Hugel Gentil

Jaboulet Crozes-Hermitage Les Jalets

Louis Jadot Château de Bellevue Morgon

Louis Jadot St-Véran

Sauvion Muscadet

Trimbach Riesling

Germany

Strub Niersteine Oelberg Kabinett

Italy

Allegrini Valpolicella Classico

Anselmi Soave

Antinori Santa Cristina Sangiovese

Bollini Trentino Pinot Grigio

Boscaini Pinot Grigio

Castello Banfi Toscana Centine

Col d'Orcia Rosso di Montalcino

Frescobaldi Chianti Rufina or Nipozzano
   Reserva

Lungarotti Rubesco

Marco Felluga Collio Pinot Grigio

Pighin Pinot Grigio

Taurino Salice Salentino

Zenato Valpolicella

New Zealand

Babich Sauvignon Blanc

Brancott Chardonnay or Sauvignon Blanc

Glazebrook Sauvignon Blanc

Kim Crawford Sauvignon Blanc

Nobilo Sauvignon Blanc

Oyster Bay Sauvignon Blanc

Saint Clair Sauvignon Blanc

Stoneleigh Chardonnay and Sauvignon Blanc

Oregon

Argyle Chardonnay

A to Z Wineworks Pinot Noir, Pinot Gris,
   Chardonnay, and Pinot Blanc

Cooper Mountain Pinot Noir

King Estate Pinot Gris

Willamette Valley Vineyards Pinot Noir

Spain

Bodegas Montecillo Crianza

Conde de Valdemar Crianza

Ports

Fonseca Bin 27

Sandeman Founders Reserve

Sparkling Wines
Bouvet Brut
Codorniu Brut Classico
Cristalino Brut
Domaine Chandon
Freixenet Brut
Gloria Ferrer Brut
Gruet
Korbel
Scharffenberger

Washington State
Columbia Crest Chardonnay, Shiraz, Merlot, and Cabernet Sauvignon
Covey Run Chardonnay and Merlot
Hogue Cabernet Sauvignon, Pinot Gris, and Merlot

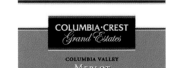

ONCE-A-MONTH WINES
($20 to $50; most under $40)

Argentina
Achaval Ferrer Malbec
Alta Vista Malbec Grand Reserva
Catena Alta Cabernet Sauvignon
Luigi Bosca Malbec Single Vineyard
Mendel Unus
Salentein Malbec

Australia
Penfolds Bin 389

California
Cabernet Sauvignon
Artesa
Beaulieu Rutherford
Beringer Knights Valley
Clos du Val
Geyser Peak Reserve
The Hess Collection

Jordan
Joseph Phelps
Louis Martini
Mondavi
Raymond
Ridge
Turnbull
Whitehall Lane

Chardonnay
Arrowood Grand Archer
Beringer Private Reserve
Chalone
Cuvaison
Ferrari-Carano
Kendall-Jackson Grand Reserve
Mondavi
Sonoma-Cutrer

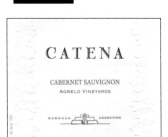

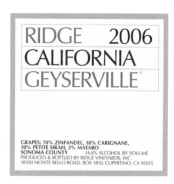

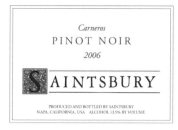

Merlot
Shafer
Clos de Bois Reverse

Pinot Noir
Acacia
Au Bon Climat
Byron
Calera
Etude
La Crema (Anderson Valley)
Mondavi
Saintsbury (Carneros)
Truchard
Williams Selyem (Sonoma Coast)

Sparkling Wine
Chandon Reserve
Domaine Carneros
Iron Horse
Roederer Estate

Syrah
Fess Parker
Four Vines
Justin

Zinfandel
Ridge Geyserville
Rosenblum (Continente)
Seghesio Old Vine

Champagne
Any non-vintage

Chile
Errazúriz Don Maximiano Founder's Reserve

France
Château Carbonnieux Blanc
Château de Malle (Sauternes)
Château de Sales
Château Fourcas-Hosten
Château Fuissé (Pouilly-Fuissé)
Château Gloria
Château Lagrezette (Cahors)
Château La Nerthe Chateauneuf-du-pape
Château Les Ormes de Pez
Château Meyney
Château Olivier Blanc
Château Phélan-Ségur
Château Pontensac
Château Sociando-Mallet
Coudoulet de Beaucastel
Domaine Leroy Bourgogne Rouge
Faiveley Mercurey
Jaboulet Crozes-Hermitage Domaine de
    Thalabert
Ladoucette Pouilly-Fumé
Marnier-Lapostolle Château de Sancerre
Olivier Leflaive Puligny-Montrachet
Pascal Jolivet Pouilly-Fumé

Germany

J.J. Prüm Wehlener Sonnenuhr Kabinett or
    Spätlese

Italy

Antinori Badia a Passignano Chianti Classico

Antinori Tenute Marchese Chianti Classico
    Riserva

Badia a Coltibuono Chianti Classico Riserva

Col d'Orcia Brunello di Montalcino

Mastroberardino Taurasi

Melini Massovecchio Chianti Classico Riserva

Ruffino Chianti Classico Riserva

New Zealand

Kim Crawford Chardonnay

Oregon

Argyle Pinot Noir

South Africa

Hamilton Russell Pinot Noir and Chardonnay

Spain

Alvaro Palacios Priorat Les Terrasses

Bodegas Montecillo Reserva

Bodegas Muga Reserva

Cune Contino Reserva

La Rioja Alta Viña Ardanza Pesquera

Marqués de Cáceres Crianza

Washington State

Chateau Ste. Michelle Chardonnay and
    Cabernet Sauvignon

Chateau Ste. Michelle Eroica Riesling

L'Ecole No. 41 Cabernet Sauvignon

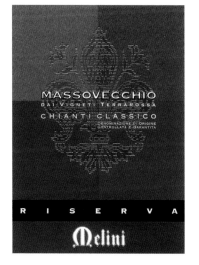

ONCE-A-YEAR WINES
($$$$+)

It's easy to buy these kinds of wine when money is no object! Any wine retailer would be more
than happy to help you spend your money!

WINES TO BUY NOW AND CELLAR FOR YOUR CHILD'S 21ST BIRTHDAY

2008 Bordeaux, Napa Cabernet Sauvignon

2007 Sauternes, Rhône (South), Napa Cabernet Sauvignon

2006 Bordeaux (Pomerol), Rhône (North), Barolo, Barbaresco, Brunello di Montalcino, German
*   (Auslese and sove), Malbec from Argentina*

2005 Bordeaux, Sauternes, Burgundy, Southern Rhône, Piedmont, Tuscany, Germany, Rioja, Ribera del Duero,
*   Southern Australia, Napa Cabernet Sauvignon, Washington Cabernet Sauvignon*

2004 Napa Cabernet Sauvignon, Piedmont

2003 Rhône (North and South), Sauternes, Bordeaux, Port

2002 Napa Cabernet Sauvignon, Germany*, Burgundy**, Sauternes

2001 Napa Cabernet Sauvignon, Sauternes, Germany*, Rioja and Ribera del Duero

2000 Bordeaux, Châteauneuf-du-Pape, Piedmont, Amarone, Port

1999 Piedmont, Rhône (North), California Zinfandel, Burgundy**

1998 Bordeaux (St-Émilion/Pomerol), Rhône (South), Piedmont (Barolo, Barbaresco)

1997 Napa Cabernet Sauvignon, Tuscany (Chianti, Brunello), Piedmont, Amarone, Port, Australian Shiraz

1996 Burgundy, Piedmont, Bordeaux (Médoc), Burgundy**, Germany*, vintage Champagne

1995 Bordeaux, Rhône, Rioja, Napa Cabernet Sauvignon, vintage Champagne

1994 Port, Napa Cabernet Sauvignon and Zinfandel, Rioja

1993 Napa Cabernet Sauvignon and Zinfandel

1992 Port, Napa Cabernet Sauvignon and Zinfandel

1991 Rhône (North), Port, Napa Cabernet Sauvignon

1990 Bordeaux, Napa Cabernet Sauvignon, Rhône, Burgundy**, Tuscany (Brunello), Piedmont, Amarone,
*   Sauternes, Champagne, Germany**

1989 Bordeaux, Rhône, Piedmont, Rioja

1988 Sauternes, Rhône (North), Piedmont

1987 Napa Cabernet Sauvignon and Zinfandel

1986 Bordeaux, Sauternes, Napa Cabernet Sauvignon

1985 Bordeaux, Port, Rhône (North), Champagne, Piedmont, Amarone

*Auslese and above **Grand Cru

VINTAGE BEST BETS

*Note: * signifies exceptional vintage, **signifies extraordinary vintage*

ARGENTINA

Mendoza: 2005*   2006**   2007   2008**

AUSTRALIA

(Barossa, Mclaren Vale, Coonawarra):

2004**   2005**   2006*   2008*

AUSTRIA

2005   2006*   2007

CALIFORNIA

Cabernet Sauvignon (Napa Valley):

1994*   1995*   1996*   1997*   1999*   2001*   2002*   2003   2004   2005*   2006*   2007**   2008

Chardonnay (By Region):

Carneros:	2002*	2003	2004*	2006	2007*	2008
Napa:	2002*	2004	2005	2006	2007*	2008
Sonoma:	2002**	2003	2004**	2005**	2006	2007*	2008
Santa Barbara:	2002*	2004	2005	2007*	2008	

Merlot (North Coast):

2002*   2003   2004*   2005*   2006   2007*   2008

Pinot Noir (By Region):

Sonoma (Carneros):	2001*	2002*	2003*	2004*	2005*	2006	2007*	2008
Santa Barbara:	2003*	2004*	2005	2007	2008		
Monterey:	2002*	2003*	2004*	2005*	2006	2007	2008

Zinfandel (North Coast):

1994*   2001*   2002   2003*   2007

Syrah:

South Central Coast:	2002*	2003*	2004*	2005	2006*	2007
North Coast:	2003	2004*	2005	2006*		

CANADA

British Columbia:	2005	2006
Ontario:	2005	2006*

CHILE

Maipo:	2005*	2007*
Casablanca:	2006	2007
Colchagua:	2005*	2007*

FRANCE

Alsace:

2001* 2002* 2003 2004 2005* 2006 2007* 2008

Beaujolais:

2002* 2003* 2005* 2006 2007 2008

Bordeaux:

"Left Bank" Médoc/St: Julien/Margaux/Pauillac/St:Estèphe/Graves:

Good Vintages:	1994	1997	1998	1999	2001	2002	2004	2006	2007	2008
Great Vintages:	1990*	1995	1996	2000*	2003	2005*			
Older Great Vintages:	1982*	1985	1986	1989					

"Right Bank" St: Émilion/Pomerol:

Good Vintages:	1995	1996	1997	1999	2002	2003	2004	2006	2007	2008

Great Vintages:	1990	1998*	2000*	2001	2005*
Older Great Vintages:	1982	1989			

Chablis:

2002* 2004 2005* 2006* 2007

Côte de Beaune (White):

1995* 1996* 2000 * 2002* 2004* 2005 * 2006* 2007 2008

Côte d'Or:

1999* 2002* 2003* 2005** 2006

Mâcon (White):

2004* 2005** 2006* 2007

Rhône Valley Wines (Red):

North: 1995 1996 1997 1998 1999* 2000 2001 2003* 2004 2005 2006* 2007 2008
South: 1995 1998* 1999 2000* 2001* 2003* 2004* 2005* 2006* 2007** 2008

Sauternes:

1986* 1988* 1989* 1990* 1995 1996 1997* 1998 2000 2001* 2002 2003*
2005* 2006 2007* 2008

The Loire Valley:
2004   2005*   2006   2007   2008

White Graves:
2000*   2005*   2006   2007*   2008

GERMANY
2001**   2002*   2003*   2004*   2005**   2006*   2007   2008

GREECE
2005   2007   2008*

ITALY
Amarone:	1990*	1993	1995*	1996	1997*	1998	2000*	2001	2002*	2003*	2005*	
Piedmont:	1990*	1996**	1997*	1998*	1999*	2000**	2001**	2003	2004**	2005*	2006*	2007
	2006*	2007										
Tuscany:	1997**	1999**	2001*	2003	2004**	2005*	2006**	2007				

NEW ZEALAND
North Island (Hawke's Bay and Martinborough): 2005   2006*   2007*   2008
South Island (Central Otago and Marlborough): 2006*   2007*   2008

OREGON
2002*   2004*   2005*   2006*   2007   2008

PORT
1963*   1970*   1977*   1983*   1985   1991*   1992*   1994*   1997*   2000*   2003*

SOUTH AFRICA (Western Cape Wines)
2005*   2006   2007   2008

SPAIN
Penedès:	2002*	2003*	2004*	2005*	2006	2007		
Priorat:	2004*	2005**	2007*					
Ribera Del Duero:	1996*	2001*	2004**	2005*	2006	2007*		
Rioja:	1994*	1995*	2001**	2003	2004**	2005*	2006	2007

TOKAY ASZÚ
2000*   2002   2003   2005*   2006*

WASHINGTON STATE
2001*   2002*   2003   2004*   2005*   2006*   2007*   2008

WINE STORAGE
AT HOME

◆

AGING WINE

DECANTING WINE

GLASSWARE

STORAGE OF WINE

I'M SURE NOT EVERYTHING YOU BOUGHT for your new wine cellar is going to be there five years from now, but some wines do improve with age, and you must protect your investment. The fun of wine collecting is trying wines at different stages in their growth.

Warmer temperatures prematurely age wine. How important is it to have proper storage for your new wine collectibles? Well, let me put it another way. Without proper storage, you will never know how good the wine could have been!

In wine collecting it seems as if it's always the cart before the horse. First I'll buy the wines, then I'll think about where I'm going to put them. Which of course is the wrong way to begin wine collecting. I've often asked my students how many of them live in châteaux and how many of them live in *apartamentos*? The *apartamento* people usually store their fine wines in the first door as you enter their *apartamento* next to their muddy shoes. If you are an apartment dweller and you have fine wine, you should look into wine storage in your area (or buy a château)!

While the optimum temperature is 55°F, I would rather the wine be a consistent 65°F all year long than swing in temperature from 55°F to 75°F. That is the worst scenario and can be very harmful to the wine. And just as warm temperatures will prematurely age the wine, temperatures too cold can freeze the wine, pushing out the cork and immediately ending the aging process.

When all else fails, especially for those living in a cozy apartment, put your wines in the refrigerator—both whites and reds—rather than risk storing them in warm conditions.

The second consideration in long-term wine storage (five years or more) is humidity. If the humidity is too low, your corks will dry out. If that happens, wine will seep out of the bottle. Again, if wine can get out, air can get in. Too much humidity, and you are likely to lose your labels. Personally, I'd rather lose my labels than lose my corks. My own wine cellar ranges from 55°F to 60°F and the humidity stays at a fairly constant 75 percent. Humidity and temperature are the most important things when it comes to wine storage, but I would also be careful of excessive vibration.

National statistics show that most wine purchased at retail stores will be consumed within three days of purchase, but for those of you who are collecting, you must protect your investment—whether you have a dozen bottles or two thousand.

Should my wines be stored horizontally or vertically?

Wine bottles should be stored horizontally, at up to a ten-degree angle, especially for long-term aging. The reason very simply is that when the bottle of wine is stored on its side, the wine will be in contact with the cork. This prevents any oxygen, the major enemy of wine, from getting into the bottle. If the wine is kept in a vertical position, the chances are great that the cork will dry out, the wine will evaporate, and the oxygen getting in will quickly spoil your wine.

P.S. Whoever wrote that it is important to turn the bottle of wine once a month was probably a beer drinker.

How long should I age my wine?

The Wall Street Journal recently came out with an article stating that most people have one or two wines that they've been saving for years for a special occasion. This is probably not a good idea! More than 90 percent of all wine—red, white, and rosé—should be consumed within a year. With that in mind, the following is a guideline to aging wine from the best producers in the best years:

WHITE

California Chardonnay	3–8+ years
French White Burgundy	2–10+ years
German Riesling	3–30+ years
(Auslese, Beerenauslese, and Trockenbeerenauslese)	
French Sauternes	3–30+ years

RED

Bordeaux Châteaux	5–30+ years
California Cabernet Sauvignon	3–15+ years

(continued on next page)

IF YOU leave a bottle of wine in a 70°F room, as opposed to a 55°F room, the wine prematurely ages at twice the normal rate.

KEVIN ZRALY'S QUICK TIPS ON TEMPERATURES FOR SERVING WINE:

1. Great Chardonnays are best at warmer temperatures (55°F to 60°F) than whites made from Sauvignon Blanc or Riesling (45°F to 55°F).
2. Champagnes and sparkling wines taste better well chilled (45°F).
3. Lighter reds, such as Gamay, Pinot Noir, Tempranillo, and Sangiovese bring out a better balance of fruit to acid when served at a cooler temperature (55°F to 60°F) than wines such as Cabernet Sauvignon and Merlot (60°F to 65°F).

SOME WINES THAT ARE READY TO DRINK IMMEDIATELY:

Riesling (dry)
Sauvignon Blanc
Pinot Grigio
Beaujolais

(continued from previous page)

RED

Argentine Malbec	3–15+ years
Barolo and Barbaresco	5–25+ years
Brunello di Montalcino	3–15+ years
Chianti Classico Riservas	3–10+ years
Spanish Riojas (Gran Reservas)	5–20+ years
Hermitage/Shiraz	5–25+ years
California Zinfandel	5–15+ years
California Merlot	2–10+ years
California/Oregon Pinot Noirs	2–5+ years
French Red Burgundy	3–8+ years
Vintage Ports	10–20+ years

There are always exceptions to the rules when it comes to generalizing about the aging of wine (especially considering the variations in vintages), hence the plus signs in the table above. I have had Bordeaux wines more than a hundred years old that were still going strong. It is also not unlikely to find a great Sauternes or Port that still needs time to age after its fiftieth birthday. But the above age spans represent more than 95 percent of the wines in their categories.

P.S. The oldest bottle of wine still aging in Bordeaux is a 1797 Lafite-Rothschild.

What's the best way to chill a bottle of wine quickly?

The best technique that I have found for chilling white wines on short notice is to submerge the bottle in a mixture of ice, water, and salt. Within ten minutes the wine is ready for drinking.

THE CORKSCREW
How many of you have seen "other people" break a cork or even push the cork in the bottle when opening wine?

Many times this happens because people either use the wrong corkscrew or they open the wine incorrectly.

Of the many different kinds of corkscrews and cork-pullers available, the most efficient and easiest tool to use is the pocket model of the Screwpull, a patented device that includes a knife and a very long screw. Simply by turning in one continuous direction, the cork is extracted effortlessly. This is the best type of corkscrew for home use, and because it is gentle, it is best for removing long, fragile corks from older wines.

The corkscrew most commonly used in restaurants is the "waiter's corkscrew." Small and flat, it contains a knife, screw, and lever, all of which fold neatly into the handle.

For opening many bottles at a time, try the "rabbit" corkscrew.

THE CORKSCREW was patented in 1795 by an Englishman who obviously wanted to enjoy his wine without having to struggle to remove the cork.

How do I open a bottle of wine?

When opening a bottle of wine, the first step is to remove the capsule. You can accomplish this best by cutting around the neck on the underside of the bottle's lip. Once you remove the capsule, wipe the top of the cork clean—often dust or mold adheres to the cork while the wine is still at the winery, and before the capsule is put on the bottle. Next, insert the screw and turn it so that it goes as deeply as possible into the cork. Don't be afraid to go through the cork. I'd rather get a little cork in my wine than not get the cork out of the bottle.

The most important technique in opening a bottle of wine comes once you have lifted the cork one-quarter of the way out. You stop lifting and turn the screw farther into the cork. Now pull the cork three-quarters of the way out. This is the point where most people feel they're in control and start pulling and bending the cork. And, of course, they end up leaving a little bit of the cork still in the bottle. The best method at this point is to use your hand to wiggle out the cork.

Just to make you feel better: I still break at least a dozen corks a year.

WHEN IN FRANCE, do as the French. My experience in visiting the French wine regions is that in Burgundy (Pinot Noir) they very rarely decant, but in Bordeaux (Cabernet Sauvignon and Merlot) they almost always decant.

MY PRIMARY reason for decanting a bottle of wine is to separate the wine from the sediment.

To Decant, Perchance to Breathe

Does a wine need to breathe?

This is one of the most controversial subjects among my wine friends, and everyone seems to have a different answer or angle regarding the question.

I think most of my peer group would agree that simply opening a bottle of wine an hour or two before service will not really help the wine. It also will not hurt the wine. It is probably a good idea if you are having a dinner party at home to open your wines before your guests arrive.

What is bothersome to me is when a waiter in a restaurant asks me whether I would like my wine to breathe before he or she serves it. A waiter once told me that the wine I had ordered needed at least thirty minutes' "breathing" before I could drink it. Not only do I disagree, but as a restaurant director, I certainly hope that the customer is ordering a second bottle thirty minutes later!

The major question still remains, though. Does a wine improve when it is taken out of the bottle and put into your decanter or glass? There are many schools of thought. I've had students swear to me that certain wines tasted much better after three hours in the decanter than when first served from the bottle. On the other hand, many studies with professional wine people have shown no discernible difference between most wines opened, poured, and consumed immediately and those that have been in a decanter over an extended period of time.

One thing for sure is that very old wine (more than twenty-five years) should be opened and consumed immediately. One of the most interesting wine experiences I ever had was early in my career, and involved a bottle of a 1945 Burgundy. When I opened the wine, the room filled with the smell of great wine. The first taste of the wine was magnificent. Unfortunately, fifteen minutes after opening the bottle, everything about the wine changed, especially the taste. The wine started losing its fruit, and the acidity overpowered the fruit.

What happened? Oxygen is the culprit here. Just as buried treasure is taken from the sea and kept in salt water to avoid exposing it to oxygen, wine is destroyed by exposure to oxygen. If I had decanted that wine first and left it to "breathe," I would never have had that first fifteen minutes of pleasure. This probably will not happen every time you open an old bottle of wine, but it is very important to be aware of how fragile older wines can be.

So what's my advice after opening thousands and thousands of bottles of wine? For me, Open it up, pour it in a glass, and enjoy the wine!

Which wines do I decant?

The three major wine collectibles are the ones that most likely will need to be decanted, especially as they get older and throw more sediment. The three major wine collectibles are:

1. Great châteaux of Bordeaux (ten years and older)
2. California Cabernets (eight years and older)
3. Vintage Port (ten years and older)

How do I decant a bottle of wine?

1. Completely remove the capsule from the neck of the bottle. This will enable you to see the wine clearly as it passes through the neck.
2. Light a candle. Most red wines are bottled in very dark green glass, making it difficult to see the wine pass through the neck of the bottle. A candle will give you the extra illumination you need and add a theatrical touch. A flashlight would do, but a candle keeps things simple.
3. Hold the decanter (a carafe or glass pitcher can also be used for this purpose) firmly in your hand.
4. Hold the wine bottle in your other hand, and gently pour the wine into the decanter while holding both over the candle at such an angle that you can see the wine pass through the neck of the bottle.
5. Continue pouring in one uninterrupted motion until you see the first signs of sediment.
6. Stop decanting once you see sediment. At this point, if there is still wine left, let it stand until the sediment settles. Then continue decanting.

GLASSWARE

Whether you're dining out or you're at home, the enjoyment of food and wine is enhanced by fine silver, china, linen, and, of course, glassware. The color of wine is as much a part of its pleasure and appeal as its bouquet and flavor. Glasses that alter or obscure the color of wine detract from

GRAND CRU CLASSÉ

1996

Château Gruaud Larose

Mis en bouteilles au Château

A SAINT-JULIEN BEYCHEVELLE (HAUT-MÉDOC) · FRANCE

SAINT-JULIEN

APPELLATION SAINT-JULIEN CONTROLÉE

RED BORDEAUX WINE

SCPF DÉSIRÉ CORDIER PROPRIÉTAIRE

CONTENTS 750 ML   PRODUCE OF FRANCE   ALC. 12.5% BY VOL.

I HAVE had good and bad experiences with decanting. I must admit that some wines did get better, but many older wines, especially when exposed to air, actually deteriorated quickly. Words of wisdom: If you decide to decant an older bottle of wine, do it immediately before service, not hours ahead of time, to make sure that the wine will not lose its flavor by being exposed to the air for an extended period of time.

the wine itself. The most suitable wineglasses are those of clear glass with a bowl large enough to allow for swirling.

A variety of shapes are available, and personal preferences should guide you when selecting glasses for home use. Some shapes, however, are better suited to certain wines than to others. For example, a smaller glass that closes in a bit at the top helps concentrate the bouquet of a white wine and also helps it keep its chill. Larger, balloon-shaped glasses are more appropriate for great red wines.

The most suitable Champagne glasses and the ones more and more restaurants are using are the tulip or the Champagne flute. These narrow glasses hold between four and eight ounces, and they allow the bubbles to rise from a single point. The tulip shape also helps to concentrate the bouquet.

How should I wash my wineglasses?

For your everyday drinking of wine, it's okay to wash your glasses in the dishwasher. But I've had many a great wine spoiled because of the detergent used. Therefore, my special wineglasses are not put into the dishwasher. They are washed by hand without any soap or detergent. Glasses are susceptible to scents, so mine are carefully dried hanging from a rack, not upside down on a counter or cloth.

THE BEST wineglasses are made by Riedel. The Riedel family of Austrian glassmakers has been on a crusade for more than 30 years to elevate wine drinking to a new level with their specially designed varietal glassware. They have designed their glasses to accentuate the best components of each grape variety. Riedel glassware comes in many different styles. The top of the line is the handcrafted Sommelier series. Next comes the Vinum. For your everyday meal—for those of you who do not want to spend a tremendous amount of money on glassware—they also produce the less expensive Overture series and the "O" wine tumbler for those of you who don't like stemware.

SELECTED GLOSSARY

Acid: One of the four components of wine. It is sometimes described as sour or tart and can be found on the sides of the tongue and mouth.

Acidification: The process of adding acid, usually tartaric or citric, to grape must before fermentation in order to boost low levels of acidity creating a more balanced wine.

Aftertaste: The sensation in the mouth that persists after the wine has been swallowed.

Alcohol: The result of fermentation whereby yeast converts the natural sugar in grapes to alcohol.

AOC: Abbreviation for Appellation d'Origine Contrôlée; the French government agency that controls wine production.

Aroma: The smell of the grapes in a wine.

Astringent: The mouthfeel created by tannins in wine.

AVA: Abbreviation for American Viticultural Area. AVAs are designated wine-producing areas in the United States.

Balance: The integration of the various components of wine such as acid, alcohol, fruit, and tannin. To be balanced, no one component should dominate the wine's taste.

Barrel-fermented: Describes wine that has been fermented in small oak barrels rather than stainless steel. The oak from a barrel will add complexity to a wine's flavor and texture.

Biodynamics: A type of holistic farming created by Rudolph Steiner in the 1920s based on the principles of organic farming—for example, compost and manure are used instead of chemical fertilizers or pesticides.

Bitter: One of the four tastes of wine, found at the back of the tongue and throat.

Blend: A combination of two or more wines or grapes, to enhance flavor, balance, and complexity.

Body: The sensation of weight of a wine in the mouth. A wine high in alcohol feels heavier than a wine with low alcohol.

Botrytis cinerea (bo-TRY-tis sin-AIR-e-a): Also called "noble rot," botrytis cinerea is a special mold that punctures the skin of a grape allowing the water to dissipate, leaving a higher than normal concentration of sugar and acid. Botrytis cinerea is necessary in making Sauternes and the rich German wines Beerenauslese and Trockenbeerenauslese.

Bouquet: The smell of a wine, influenced by winemaking processes and barrel aging.

Brix (bricks): A scale that measures the sugar level of the unfermented grape juice.

Agiorgitiko (Greece)
Barbera (Italy, California)
Blaufränkisch (Austria)
Cabernet Franc (Bordeaux, Canada, Loire Valley)
Cabernet Sauvignon (Argentina, Australia, Bordeaux, California, Canada, Chile, Hungary, South Africa, Spain, Washington)
Cariñena (Spain)
Carménère (Chile)
Cinsault (Rhône Valley)
Concord (United States)
Gamay (Burgundy)
Garnacha/Grenache (Spain/France)
Kadarka (Hungary)
Kékfrankos (Hungary)
Malbec (Argentina)
Merlot (Argentina, Bordeaux, California, Canada, Chile, Hungary, Spain, Washington)
Monastrell (Spain)
Nebbiolo (Piedmont)
Petite Syrah (California)
Pinot Meunier (Champagne)
Pinot Noir (Austria, Burgundy, California, Canada, Hungary, New Zealand, Oregon)
Portugieser (Hungary)
Sangiovese (Tuscany)
St. Laurent (Austria)
Syrah/Shiraz (Argentina, California, Canada, Chile, Rhone Valley, South Africa, Spain, Washington/Australia)
Tempranillo (Spain, Argentina)
Xinomavro (Greece)
Zinfandel (California)

Brut: A French term used for the driest style of Champagne and/or sparkling wine.

Chaptalization: The addition of sugar to the must before fermentation to increase the alcohol level of the finished wine.

Character: Refers to the aspects of the wine typical of its grape varieties, or the overall characteristics of the wine.

Classified châteaux: The châteaux in the Bordeaux region of France that are known to produce the best wine.

Colheita (coal-AY-ta): Means "vintage" in Portuguese.

Components: The components of a wine make up its character, style, and taste. Some components are: acidity, alcohol, fruit, tannin, and residual sugar.

Cru: Certain vineyards in France are designated grand cru and premier cru, the classification indicating level of quality.

Cuvée: From the French cuve (vat); may refer to a particular blend of grapes or, in Champagne, to the select portion of the juice from the pressing of the grapes.

Decanting: The process of pouring wine from its bottle into a carafe to separate the sediment from the wine.

Dégorgement (day-gorzh-MOWN): One step of the Champagne method (méthode champenoise) used to expel the sediment from the bottle.

Demi-sec (deh-mee SECK): A Champagne containing a higher level of residual sugar than a brut.

DOC: Abbreviation for Denominazione di Origine Controllata, the Italian government agency that controls wine production. Spain also uses this abbreviation for Denominación de Origen Condado.

DOCG: Abbreviation for Denominazione di Origine Controllata e Garantita; the Italian government allows this marking to appear only on the finest Italian wines. The G stands for "guaranteed."

Dosage (doh-SAHZH): The addition of sugar, often mixed with wine or brandy, in the final step in the production of Champagne or sparkling wine.

Drip irrigation: System for watering vines that applies water directly to the roots through a network of emitters or microsprayers; drip irrigation conserves water and nutrients and minimizes erosion.

Dry: Wine containing very little residual sugar. It is the opposite of sweet, in wine terms.

Estate-bottled: Wine that is made, produced, and bottled on the estate where the grapes were grown.

Extra dry: Less dry than brut Champagne.

Fermentation: The process of transforming sugar into alcohol in the presence of yeast, turning grape juice into wine.

Filtration: Removal of yeasts and other solids from a wine before bottling to clarify and stabilize the wine.

Fino (FEE-noh): A type of Sherry.

Finish: The taste and feel that wine leaves in the mouth after swallowing. Some wines disappear immediately while others can linger for some time.

First growth: The five highest-quality Bordeaux châteaux wines from the Médoc Classification of 1855.

Flor: A type of yeast that develops in some Sherry production.

Fortified wine: A wine such as Port or Sherry that has additional grape spirits (brandy, for example) added to raise the alcohol content.

Fruit: One of the components of wine that derives from the grape itself.

Grand Cru (grawn crew): The highest classification for wines in Burgundy.

Grand Cru Classé (grawn crew clas-SAY): The highest level of the Bordeaux classification.

Gran Reserva: A Spanish wine that has had extra aging.

Hectare: A metric measure of area that equals 2.471 acres.

Hectoliter: A metric measure of volume that equals 26.42 U.S. gallons.

Halbtrocken: The German term meaning "semidry."

Kabinett (kah-bee-NETT): A light, semi-dry German wine.

Maceration: The chemical process by which tannin, color, and flavor are extracted from the grape skins into the wine. Temperature and alcohol content influence the speed at which maceration occurs.

Malolactic fermentation: A secondary fermentation process wherein malic acid is converted into lactic acid and carbon dioxide. This process reduces the wine's acidity and adds complexity.

Mechanical harvester: A machine used on flat vineyards. It shakes the vines to harvest the grapes.

Meritage: Trademark designation for specific high-quality American wines containing the same blend of varieties that are used in the making of Bordeaux wines in France.

Méthode Champenoise (may-TUD shahm-pen-WAHZ): The method by which Champagne is made. This method is also used in other parts of the world to produce sparkling wines.

Mouthfeel: Sensation of texture in the mouth when tasting wine, e.g., smooth, or tannic.

Must: Unfermented grape juice extracted during the crushing process.

"Noble Rot": See Botrytis cinerea.

Nose: The term used to describe the bouquet and aroma of wine.

Phenolics: Chemical compounds derived especially but not only from the skins, stems, and seeds of grapes that affect the color and flavor of wine. Tannin is one example. Maceration can increase their presence in wines.

Oenology: The science and scientific study of winemaking.

Phylloxera (fill-LOCK-she-rah): A root louse that kills grape vines.

HERE IS A LIST OF WHITE GRAPE VARIETALS, AND SOME OF THE REGIONS WHERE THEY CAN BE FOUND:

Albariño (Spain)

Assyrtiko (Greece)

Chardonnay (Argentina, Australia, Austria, Burgundy, Canada, Chile, Hungary, New Zealand, Oregon, South Africa, Spain, United States)

Chenin Blanc (California, Loire Valley, South Africa)

Furmint (Hungary)

Gewürztraminer (Alsace, Germany)

Grüner Veltliner (Austria)

Hárslevel (Hungary)

Macabeo (Spain)

Moschofilero (Greece)

Olaszrizling (Hungary)

Pinot Blanc (Alsace)

Pinot Grigio/Pinot Gris (Italy/Canada, France, Hungary, United States)

Riesling (Alsace, Austria, Canada, United States)

Roditis (Greece)

Sauvignon Blanc (California, Chile, Graves, Loire Valley, New Zealand, Sauternes, South Africa)

Semillon (Australia, Graves, Sauternes)

Szürkebarát (Hungary)

Torrontés Riojano (Argentina)

Trebbiano (Italy)

Verdejo (Spain)

Vidal (Canada)

Viognier (California, Rhône Valley)

Praedikatswein (pray-dee-KAHTS-vine): The highest level of quality in German wines.

Premier Cru: A wine that has special characteristics that comes from a specific designated vineyard in Burgundy, France, or is blended from several such vineyards.

Proprietary wine: A wine that's given a brand name like any other product and is marketed as such, e.g., Riunite, Mouton-Cadet.

Qualitätswein (kval-ee-TATES-vine): A German term meaning "quality wine."

Residual sugar: Any unfermented sugar that remains in a finished wine. Residual sugar determines how dry or sweet a wine is.

Riddling: One step of the Champagne-making process in which the bottles are turned gradually each day for weeks until they are upside down, so that the sediment rests in the neck of the bottle.

Sediment: Particulate matter that accumulates in wine as it ages.

Sommelier (so-mel-YAY): The French term for cellarmaster, or wine steward.

Sulfur dioxide: A substance used in winemaking and grape growing as a preservative, an antioxidant, and also as a sterilizing agent.

Tannin: One of the components of wine, tannin is a natural compound and preservative that comes from the skins, stems, and pips of the grapes and also from the wood barrel in which wine is aged.

Terroir: A French term for all of the elements that contribute to the distinctive characteristics of a particular vineyard site that include its soil, subsoil, slope, drainage, elevation, and climate including exposure to the sun, temperature and precipitation.

Varietal wine: A wine that is labeled with the predominant grape used to produce the wine. For example, a wine made from Chardonnay grapes would be labeled "Chardonnay."

Vintage: The year the grapes are harvested.

Vinification: Winemaking.

Vitis labrusca (VEE-tiss la-BREW-skah): A native grape species in America.

Vitis vinifera (VEE-tiss vih-NIFF-er-ah): The grape species that is used in most countries in the world for winemaking.

HOW TO USE THE TASTING NOTES

THE MORE YOU CAN WRITE ABOUT A WINE at the time you are tasting it, the better! It will definitely help you become a smarter buyer by understanding your own likes and dislikes.

At the top of the tasting notes in this journal, the country, region, vintage, and producer are self-explanatory. The 60-second wine tasting is explained on pages 28 and 29. I discuss residual sugar, acid, tannin, and fruit on pages 24 and 25. Since everyone has a different threshold for these wine components, it is very important to fill in this box with your own impressions—were they low, medium, or high to your individual taste?

The color of a wine can tell you many things about the wine before you smell or taste it. To understand the different colors associated with wine, see pages 16 and 17. Understanding a wine's texture as in light, medium, or full-bodied will help you determine your style of wine.

Hopefully you have bought more than one bottle of the wine to taste, especially if you think the wines needs more time to age. The fun part is watching a wine change the balance of its components over a period of time.

Finally, you should set-up your own rating system. *Wine Spectator* and Robert Parker use a 100-point system to rate their wines. *The New York Times* uses a one to four star rating. *Decanter* magazine out of the U.K. has one to five bottles, five being the best wine. Whatever system you choose, keep in mind that it is actually the most important part of your tasting notes. I go back to my own ratings from years ago to see how I have improved in my own tasting abilities.

HOW TO TAKE A WINE LABEL OFF A BOTTLE

This is one of the most frequently asked questions by my students and of course, very important for this journal. The labels will bring back memories of particular wines and who you enjoyed them with. They will also give you valuable information about the wine.

When I began my wine journey many years ago, the only way to get the label off was to soak the wine bottle in a bucket of warm water and hope that the winery used a glue that didn't cement the label to the bottle! This method still works most of the time, but today you can actually buy an adhesive, appropriately called, "Label Savers" which you attach to the bottle over the label and peel it off. You can buy these at www.wineappreciationguild.com.

Of course, in today's digital world, you can also just take a picture of the label without the mess of a bucket of water—it's a lot easier too!

TASTING NOTES

Country: _____   Region: _____   Vintage: _____   Producer: _____

60 Second Wine Tasting:

0-15 _____

_____

15-30 _____

30-45 _____

45-60 _____

_____

	Low	Medium	High
Residual Sugar			
Fruit			
Acid			
Tannin			

Color: _____

Aroma/Bouquet: _____

_____

_____

_____

Light-Bodied ☐   Medium-Bodied ☐   Full-Bodied ☐

Ageability:
Ready to drink? ☐   Needs more time? ☐   Past its prime? ☐

Cost: _____   Date Purchased: _____   Where Purchased: _____

Personal Ratings/Comments: _____

_____

_____

_____

Date: _____

WINE LABELS

TASTING NOTES

Country: _____ Region: _____ Vintage: _____ Producer: _____

60 Second Wine Tasting:

0-15 _____

_____

15-30 _____

_____

30-45 _____

_____

45-60 _____

_____

	Low	Medium	High
Residual Sugar			
Fruit			
Acid			
Tannin			

Color: _____

Aroma/Bouquet: _____

_____

_____

_____

Light-Bodied ☐   Medium-Bodied ☐   Full-Bodied ☐

Ageability:
Ready to drink? ☐   Needs more time? ☐   Past its prime? ☐

Cost: _____ Date Purchased: _____ Where Purchased: _____

Personal Ratings/Comments: _____

_____

_____

_____

Date: _____

WINE LABELS

TASTING NOTES

Country: _____   Region: _____   Vintage: _____   Producer: _____

60 Second Wine Tasting:

0-15 _____

_____

15-30 _____

_____

30-45 _____

_____

45-60 _____

_____

	Low	Medium	High
Residual Sugar			
Fruit			
Acid			
Tannin			

Color: _____

Aroma/Bouquet: _____

_____

_____

_____

Light-Bodied ☐   Medium-Bodied ☐   Full-Bodied ☐

Ageability:
Ready to drink? ☐   Needs more time? ☐   Past its prime? ☐

Cost: _____   Date Purchased: _____   Where Purchased: _____

Personal Ratings/Comments: _____

_____

_____

_____

Date: _____

TASTING NOTES

Country: _____ Region: _____ Vintage: _____ Producer: _____

60 Second Wine Tasting:

0-15 _____
_____

15-30 _____
_____

30-45 _____
_____

45-60 _____
_____

	Low	Medium	High
Residual Sugar			
Fruit			
Acid			
Tannin			

Color: _____
Aroma/Bouquet: _____
_____
_____
_____

Light-Bodied ☐   Medium-Bodied ☐   Full-Bodied ☐

Ageability:
Ready to drink? ☐   Needs more time? ☐   Past its prime? ☐

Cost: _____ Date Purchased: _____ Where Purchased: _____

Personal Ratings/Comments: _____

_____

_____

_____

Date: _____

TASTING NOTES

Country: _____   Region: _____   Vintage: _____   Producer: _____

60 Second Wine Tasting:

0-15 _____

_____

15-30 _____

30-45 _____

_____

45-60 _____

_____

	Low	Medium	High
Residual Sugar			
Fruit			
Acid			
Tannin			

Color: _____
Aroma/Bouquet: _____

_____

_____

Light-Bodied ☐   Medium-Bodied ☐   Full-Bodied ☐

Ageability:
Ready to drink? ☐   Needs more time? ☐   Past its prime? ☐

Cost: _____   Date Purchased: _____   Where Purchased: _____

Personal Ratings/Comments: _____

_____

_____

_____

Date: _____

WINE LABELS

TASTING NOTES

Country: _____   Region: _____   Vintage: _____   Producer: _____

60 Second Wine Tasting:

0-15 _____

_____

15-30 _____

_____

30-45 _____

_____

45-60 _____

_____

	Low	Medium	High
Residual Sugar			
Fruit			
Acid			
Tannin			

Color: _____

Aroma/Bouquet: _____

_____

_____

_____

Light-Bodied ☐   Medium-Bodied ☐   Full-Bodied ☐

Ageability:
Ready to drink? ☐   Needs more time? ☐   Past its prime? ☐

Cost: _____   Date Purchased: _____   Where Purchased: _____

Personal Ratings/Comments: _____

_____

_____

_____

Date: _____

TASTING NOTES

Country: _____   Region: _____   Vintage: _____   Producer: _____

60 Second Wine Tasting:

0-15 _____

_____

15-30 _____

_____

30-45 _____

_____

45-60 _____

_____

	Low	Medium	High
Residual Sugar			
Fruit			
Acid			
Tannin			

Color: _____

Aroma/Bouquet: _____

_____

_____

_____

Light-Bodied ☐   Medium-Bodied ☐   Full-Bodied ☐

Ageability:

Ready to drink? ☐   Needs more time? ☐   Past its prime? ☐

Cost: _____   Date Purchased: _____   Where Purchased: _____

Personal Ratings/Comments: _____

_____

_____

_____

Date: _____

TASTING NOTES

Country: _____   Region: _____   Vintage: _____   Producer: _____

60 Second Wine Tasting:

0-15 _____

_____

15-30 _____

_____

30-45 _____

_____

45-60 _____

_____

	Low	Medium	High
Residual Sugar			
Fruit			
Acid			
Tannin			

Color: _____

Aroma/Bouquet: _____

_____

_____

_____

Light-Bodied ☐   Medium-Bodied ☐   Full-Bodied ☐

Ageability:

Ready to drink? ☐   Needs more time? ☐   Past its prime? ☐

Cost: _____   Date Purchased: _____   Where Purchased: _____

Personal Ratings/Comments: _____

_____

_____

_____

Date: _____

TASTING NOTES

Country: _____ Region: _____ Vintage: _____ Producer: _____

60 Second Wine Tasting:

0-15 _____
_____

15-30 _____

30-45 _____
_____

45-60 _____
_____

	Low	Medium	High
Residual Sugar			
Fruit			
Acid			
Tannin			

Color: _____

Aroma/Bouquet: _____
_____
_____
_____

Light-Bodied ☐   Medium-Bodied ☐   Full-Bodied ☐

Ageability:
Ready to drink? ☐   Needs more time? ☐   Past its prime? ☐

Cost: _____ Date Purchased: _____ Where Purchased: _____

Personal Ratings/Comments: _____

_____

_____

_____

Date: _____

WINE LABELS

TASTING NOTES

Country: _____ Region: _____ Vintage: _____ Producer: _____

60 Second Wine Tasting:

0-15 _____

_____

15-30 _____

_____

30-45 _____

_____

45-60 _____

_____

	Low	Medium	High
Residual Sugar			
Fruit			
Acid			
Tannin			

Color: _____

Aroma/Bouquet: _____

_____

_____

_____

Light-Bodied ☐   Medium-Bodied ☐   Full-Bodied ☐

Ageability:

Ready to drink? ☐   Needs more time? ☐   Past its prime? ☐

Cost: _____ Date Purchased: _____ Where Purchased: _____

Personal Ratings/Comments: _____

_____

_____

_____

Date: _____

TASTING NOTES

Country: _____   Region: _____   Vintage: _____   Producer: _____

60 Second Wine Tasting:

0-15 _____

_____

15-30 _____

_____

30-45 _____

_____

45-60 _____

_____

	Low	Medium	High
Residual Sugar			
Fruit			
Acid			
Tannin			

Color: _____

Aroma/Bouquet: _____

_____

_____

_____

Light-Bodied ☐   Medium-Bodied ☐   Full-Bodied ☐

Ageability:
Ready to drink? ☐   Needs more time? ☐   Past its prime? ☐

Cost: _____   Date Purchased: _____   Where Purchased: _____

Personal Ratings/Comments: _____

_____

_____

_____

Date: _____

TASTING NOTES

Country: _____   Region: _____   Vintage: _____   Producer: _____

60 Second Wine Tasting:

0-15 _____

_____

15-30 _____

_____

30-45 _____

_____

45-60 _____

_____

	Low	Medium	High
Residual Sugar			
Fruit			
Acid			
Tannin			

Color: _____

Aroma/Bouquet: _____

_____

_____

_____

Light-Bodied ☐   Medium-Bodied ☐   Full-Bodied ☐

Ageability:

Ready to drink? ☐   Needs more time? ☐   Past its prime? ☐

Cost: _____   Date Purchased: _____   Where Purchased: _____

Personal Ratings/Comments: _____

_____

_____

_____

Date: _____

TASTING NOTES

Country: _____ Region: _____ Vintage: _____ Producer: _____

60 Second Wine Tasting:

0-15 _____

_____

15-30 _____

_____

30-45 _____

_____

45-60 _____

_____

	Low	Medium	High
Residual Sugar			
Fruit			
Acid			
Tannin			

Color: _____

Aroma/Bouquet: _____

_____

_____

_____

Light-Bodied ☐

Medium-Bodied ☐

Full-Bodied ☐

Ageability:

Ready to drink? ☐

Needs more time? ☐

Past its prime? ☐

Cost: _____ Date Purchased: _____ Where Purchased: _____

Personal Ratings/Comments: _____

_____

_____

_____

Date: _____

TASTING NOTES

Country: _____ Region: _____ Vintage: _____ Producer: _____

60 Second Wine Tasting:

0-15 _____

_____

15-30 _____

_____

30-45 _____

45-60 _____

_____

	Low	Medium	High
Residual Sugar			
Fruit			
Acid			
Tannin			

Color: _____

Aroma/Bouquet: _____

_____

_____

_____

Light-Bodied ☐   Medium-Bodied ☐   Full-Bodied ☐

Ageability:

Ready to drink? ☐   Needs more time? ☐   Past its prime? ☐

Cost: _____ Date Purchased: _____ Where Purchased: _____

Personal Ratings/Comments: _____

_____

_____

_____

Date: _____

TASTING NOTES

Country: _____ Region: _____ Vintage: _____ Producer: _____

60 Second Wine Tasting:

0-15 _____

_____

15-30 _____

30-45 _____

_____

45-60 _____

_____

	Low	Medium	High
Residual Sugar			
Fruit			
Acid			
Tannin			

Color: _____

Aroma/Bouquet: _____

_____

_____

_____

Light-Bodied ☐   Medium-Bodied ☐   Full-Bodied ☐

Ageability:

Ready to drink? ☐   Needs more time? ☐   Past its prime? ☐

Cost: _____ Date Purchased: _____ Where Purchased: _____

Personal Ratings/Comments: _____

_____

_____

_____

Date: _____

TASTING NOTES

Country: _____ Region: _____ Vintage: _____ Producer: _____

60 Second Wine Tasting:

0-15 _____

_____

15-30 _____

30-45 _____

_____

45-60 _____

_____

	Low	Medium	High
Residual Sugar			
Fruit			
Acid			
Tannin			

Color: _____

Aroma/Bouquet: _____

_____

_____

_____

Light-Bodied ☐   Medium-Bodied ☐   Full-Bodied ☐

Ageability:
Ready to drink? ☐   Needs more time? ☐   Past its prime? ☐

Cost: _____ Date Purchased: _____ Where Purchased: _____

Personal Ratings/Comments: _____

_____

_____

_____

Date: _____

TASTING NOTES

Country: _____ Region: _____ Vintage: _____ Producer: _____

60 Second Wine Tasting:

0-15 _____

_____

15-30 _____

30-45 _____

_____

45-60 _____

_____

	Low	Medium	High
Residual Sugar			
Fruit			
Acid			
Tannin			

Color: _____

Aroma/Bouquet: _____

_____

_____

_____

Light-Bodied ☐   Medium-Bodied ☐   Full-Bodied ☐

Ageability:

Ready to drink? ☐   Needs more time? ☐   Past its prime? ☐

Cost: _____   Date Purchased: _____   Where Purchased: _____

Personal Ratings/Comments: _____

_____

_____

_____

Date: _____

TASTING NOTES

Country: _____ Region: _____ Vintage: _____ Producer: _____

60 Second Wine Tasting:

0-15 _____

_____

15-30 _____

_____

30-45 _____

_____

45-60 _____

_____

	Low	Medium	High
Residual Sugar			
Fruit			
Acid			
Tannin			

Color: _____

Aroma/Bouquet: _____

_____

_____

Light-Bodied ☐   Medium-Bodied ☐   Full-Bodied ☐

Ageability:
Ready to drink? ☐   Needs more time? ☐   Past its prime? ☐

Cost: _____ Date Purchased: _____ Where Purchased: _____

Personal Ratings/Comments: _____

_____

_____

_____

Date: _____

TASTING NOTES

Country: _____   Region: _____   Vintage: _____   Producer: _____

60 Second Wine Tasting:

0-15 _____

_____

15-30 _____

_____

30-45 _____

_____

45-60 _____

_____

	Low	Medium	High
Residual Sugar			
Fruit			
Acid			
Tannin			

Color: _____

Aroma/Bouquet: _____

_____

_____

_____

Light-Bodied ☐   Medium-Bodied ☐   Full-Bodied ☐

Ageability:
Ready to drink? ☐   Needs more time? ☐   Past its prime? ☐

Cost: _____   Date Purchased: _____   Where Purchased: _____

Personal Ratings/Comments: _____

_____

_____

_____

Date: _____

WINE LABELS

TASTING NOTES

Country: _____   Region: _____   Vintage: _____   Producer: _____

60 Second Wine Tasting:

0-15 _____

_____

15-30 _____

30-45 _____

45-60 _____

_____

	Low	Medium	High
Residual Sugar			
Fruit			
Acid			
Tannin			

Color: _____

Aroma/Bouquet: _____

_____

_____

_____

Light-Bodied ☐   Medium-Bodied ☐   Full-Bodied ☐

Ageability:
Ready to drink? ☐   Needs more time? ☐   Past its prime? ☐

Cost: _____   Date Purchased: _____   Where Purchased: _____

Personal Ratings/Comments: _____

_____

_____

_____

Date: _____

TASTING NOTES

Country: _____   Region: _____   Vintage: _____   Producer: _____

60 Second Wine Tasting:

0-15 _____
_____

15-30 _____
_____

30-45 _____
_____

45-60 _____
_____

	Low	Medium	High
Residual Sugar			
Fruit			
Acid			
Tannin			

Color: _____

Aroma/Bouquet: _____
_____
_____
_____

Light-Bodied ☐   Medium-Bodied ☐   Full-Bodied ☐

Ageability:
Ready to drink? ☐   Needs more time? ☐   Past its prime? ☐

Cost: _____   Date Purchased: _____   Where Purchased: _____

Personal Ratings/Comments: _____
_____
_____
_____

Date: _____

TASTING NOTES

Country: _____ Region: _____ Vintage: _____ Producer: _____

60 Second Wine Tasting:

0-15 _____

_____

15-30 _____

_____

30-45 _____

_____

45-60 _____

_____

	Low	Medium	High
Residual Sugar			
Fruit			
Acid			
Tannin			

Color: _____

Aroma/Bouquet: _____

_____

_____

_____

Light-Bodied ☐   Medium-Bodied ☐   Full-Bodied ☐

Ageability:
Ready to drink? ☐   Needs more time? ☐   Past its prime? ☐

Cost: _____ Date Purchased: _____ Where Purchased: _____

Personal Ratings/Comments: _____

_____

_____

_____

Date: _____

WINE LABELS

TASTING NOTES

Country: _____   Region: _____   Vintage: _____   Producer: _____

60 Second Wine Tasting:

0-15 _____
_____

15-30 _____
_____

30-45 _____
_____

45-60 _____
_____

	Low	Medium	High
Residual Sugar			
Fruit			
Acid			
Tannin			

Color: _____

Aroma/Bouquet: _____
_____
_____
_____

Light-Bodied ☐   Medium-Bodied ☐   Full-Bodied ☐

Ageability:
Ready to drink? ☐   Needs more time? ☐   Past its prime? ☐

Cost: _____   Date Purchased: _____   Where Purchased: _____

Personal Ratings/Comments: _____
_____
_____
_____

Date: _____

TASTING NOTES

Country: _____   Region: _____   Vintage: _____   Producer: _____

60 Second Wine Tasting:

0-15 _____

_____

15-30 _____

_____

30-45 _____

_____

45-60 _____

_____

	Low	Medium	High
Residual Sugar			
Fruit			
Acid			
Tannin			

Color: _____

Aroma/Bouquet: _____

_____

_____

_____

Light-Bodied ☐   Medium-Bodied ☐   Full-Bodied ☐

Ageability:

Ready to drink? ☐   Needs more time? ☐   Past its prime? ☐

Cost: _____   Date Purchased: _____   Where Purchased: _____

Personal Ratings/Comments: _____

_____

_____

_____

Date: _____

TASTING NOTES

Country: _____   Region: _____   Vintage: _____   Producer: _____

60 Second Wine Tasting:

0-15 _____

_____

15-30 _____

30-45 _____

_____

45-60 _____

_____

	Low	Medium	High
Residual Sugar			
Fruit			
Acid			
Tannin			

Color: _____

Aroma/Bouquet: _____

_____

_____

_____

Light-Bodied ☐   Medium-Bodied ☐   Full-Bodied ☐

Ageability:

Ready to drink? ☐   Needs more time? ☐   Past its prime? ☐

Cost: _____   Date Purchased: _____   Where Purchased: _____

Personal Ratings/Comments: _____

_____

_____

_____

Date: _____

TASTING NOTES

Country: _____   Region: _____   Vintage: _____   Producer: _____

60 Second Wine Tasting:

0-15 _____

_____

15-30 _____

_____

30-45 _____

_____

45-60 _____

_____

	Low	Medium	High
Residual Sugar			
Fruit			
Acid			
Tannin			

Color: _____

Aroma/Bouquet: _____

_____

_____

Light-Bodied ☐   Medium-Bodied ☐   Full-Bodied ☐

Ageability:
Ready to drink? ☐   Needs more time? ☐   Past its prime? ☐

Cost: _____   Date Purchased: _____   Where Purchased: _____

Personal Ratings/Comments: _____

_____

_____

_____

Date: _____

TASTING NOTES

Country: _____   Region: _____   Vintage: _____   Producer: _____

60 Second Wine Tasting:

0-15 _____

_____

15-30 _____

_____

30-45 _____

_____

45-60 _____

_____

	Low	Medium	High
Residual Sugar			
Fruit			
Acid			
Tannin			

Color: _____

Aroma/Bouquet: _____

_____

_____

_____

Light-Bodied ☐   Medium-Bodied ☐   Full-Bodied ☐

Ageability:
Ready to drink? ☐   Needs more time? ☐   Past its prime? ☐

Cost: _____   Date Purchased: _____   Where Purchased: _____

Personal Ratings/Comments: _____

_____

_____

_____

Date: _____

TASTING NOTES

Country: _____   Region: _____   Vintage: _____   Producer: _____

60 Second Wine Tasting:

0-15 _____
_____

15-30 _____
_____

30-45 _____
_____

45-60 _____
_____

	Low	Medium	High
Residual Sugar			
Fruit			
Acid			
Tannin			

Color: _____

Aroma/Bouquet: _____

_____

_____

_____

Light-Bodied ☐   Medium-Bodied ☐   Full-Bodied ☐

Ageability:
Ready to drink? ☐   Needs more time? ☐   Past its prime? ☐

Cost: _____   Date Purchased: _____   Where Purchased: _____

Personal Ratings/Comments: _____

_____

_____

_____

Date: _____

TASTING NOTES

Country: _____ Region: _____ Vintage: _____ Producer: _____

60 Second Wine Tasting:

0-15 _____

_____

15-30 _____

_____

30-45 _____

_____

45-60 _____

_____

	Low	Medium	High
Residual Sugar			
Fruit			
Acid			
Tannin			

Color: _____

Aroma/Bouquet: _____

_____

_____

Light-Bodied ☐   Medium-Bodied ☐   Full-Bodied ☐

Ageability:
Ready to drink? ☐   Needs more time? ☐   Past its prime? ☐

Cost: _____ Date Purchased: _____ Where Purchased: _____

Personal Ratings/Comments: _____

_____

_____

_____

Date: _____

TASTING NOTES

Country: _____ Region: _____ Vintage: _____ Producer: _____

60 Second Wine Tasting:

0-15 _____

_____

15-30 _____

_____

30-45 _____

_____

45-60 _____

_____

	Low	Medium	High
Residual Sugar			
Fruit			
Acid			
Tannin			

Color: _____

Aroma/Bouquet: _____

_____

_____

_____

Light-Bodied ☐   Medium-Bodied ☐   Full-Bodied ☐

Ageability:

Ready to drink? ☐   Needs more time? ☐   Past its prime? ☐

Cost: _____ Date Purchased: _____ Where Purchased: _____

Personal Ratings/Comments: _____

_____

_____

_____

Date: _____

TASTING NOTES

Country: _____   Region: _____   Vintage: _____   Producer: _____

60 Second Wine Tasting:

0-15 _____

_____

15-30 _____

_____

30-45 _____

_____

45-60 _____

_____

	Low	Medium	High
Residual Sugar			
Fruit			
Acid			
Tannin			

Color: _____

Aroma/Bouquet: _____

_____

_____

_____

Light-Bodied ☐   Medium-Bodied ☐   Full-Bodied ☐

Ageability:
Ready to drink? ☐   Needs more time? ☐   Past its prime? ☐

Cost: _____   Date Purchased: _____   Where Purchased: _____

Personal Ratings/Comments: _____

_____

_____

_____

Date: _____

TASTING NOTES

Country: _____   Region: _____   Vintage: _____   Producer: _____

60 Second Wine Tasting:

0-15 _____

_____

15-30 _____

_____

30-45 _____

_____

45-60 _____

_____

	Low	Medium	High
Residual Sugar			
Fruit			
Acid			
Tannin			

Color: _____

Aroma/Bouquet: _____

_____

_____

_____

Light-Bodied ☐   Medium-Bodied ☐   Full-Bodied ☐

Ageability:
Ready to drink? ☐   Needs more time? ☐   Past its prime? ☐

Cost: _____   Date Purchased: _____   Where Purchased: _____

Personal Ratings/Comments: _____

_____

_____

_____

Date: _____

TASTING NOTES

Country: _____   Region: _____   Vintage: _____   Producer: _____

60 Second Wine Tasting:

0-15 _____

_____

15-30 _____

_____

30-45 _____

_____

45-60 _____

_____

	Low	Medium	High
Residual Sugar			
Fruit			
Acid			
Tannin			

Color: _____

Aroma/Bouquet: _____

_____

_____

Light-Bodied ☐   Medium-Bodied ☐   Full-Bodied ☐

Ageability:
Ready to drink? ☐   Needs more time? ☐   Past its prime? ☐

Cost: _____   Date Purchased: _____   Where Purchased: _____

Personal Ratings/Comments: _____

_____

_____

_____

Date: _____

TASTING NOTES

Country: _____   Region: _____   Vintage: _____   Producer: _____

60 Second Wine Tasting:

0-15 _____

_____

15-30 _____

_____

30-45 _____

_____

45-60 _____

_____

	Low	Medium	High
Residual Sugar			
Fruit			
Acid			
Tannin			

Color: _____

Aroma/Bouquet: _____

_____

_____

_____

Light-Bodied ☐   Medium-Bodied ☐   Full-Bodied ☐

Ageability:
Ready to drink? ☐   Needs more time? ☐   Past its prime? ☐

Cost: _____   Date Purchased: _____   Where Purchased: _____

Personal Ratings/Comments: _____

_____

_____

_____

Date: _____

WINE LABELS

TASTING NOTES

Country: _____   Region: _____   Vintage: _____   Producer: _____

60 Second Wine Tasting:

0-15 _____

_____

15-30 _____

30-45 _____

_____

45-60 _____

_____

	Low	Medium	High
Residual Sugar			
Fruit			
Acid			
Tannin			

Color: _____

Aroma/Bouquet: _____

_____

_____

_____

Light-Bodied ☐   Medium-Bodied ☐   Full-Bodied ☐

Ageability:
Ready to drink? ☐   Needs more time? ☐   Past its prime? ☐

Cost: _____   Date Purchased: _____   Where Purchased: _____

Personal Ratings/Comments: _____

_____

_____

_____

Date: _____

TASTING NOTES

Country: _____   Region: _____   Vintage: _____   Producer: _____

60 Second Wine Tasting:

0-15 _____

_____

15-30 _____

30-45 _____

_____

45-60 _____

_____

	Low	Medium	High
Residual Sugar			
Fruit			
Acid			
Tannin			

Color: _____

Aroma/Bouquet: _____

_____

_____

_____

Light-Bodied ☐   Medium-Bodied ☐   Full-Bodied ☐

Ageability:

Ready to drink? ☐   Needs more time? ☐   Past its prime? ☐

Cost: _____   Date Purchased: _____   Where Purchased: _____

Personal Ratings/Comments: _____

_____

_____

_____

Date: _____

TASTING NOTES

Country: _____   Region: _____   Vintage: _____   Producer: _____

60 Second Wine Tasting:

0-15 _____

_____

15-30 _____

_____

30-45 _____

_____

45-60 _____

_____

	Low	Medium	High
Residual Sugar			
Fruit			
Acid			
Tannin			

Color: _____

Aroma/Bouquet: _____

_____

_____

_____

Light-Bodied ☐   Medium-Bodied ☐   Full-Bodied ☐

Ageability:
Ready to drink? ☐   Needs more time? ☐   Past its prime? ☐

Cost: _____   Date Purchased: _____   Where Purchased: _____

Personal Ratings/Comments: _____

_____

_____

_____

Date: _____

TASTING NOTES

Country: _____   Region: _____   Vintage: _____   Producer: _____

60 Second Wine Tasting:

0-15 _____

_____

15-30 _____

_____

30-45 _____

45-60 _____

	Low	Medium	High
Residual Sugar			
Fruit			
Acid			
Tannin			

Color: _____

Aroma/Bouquet: _____

_____

_____

Light-Bodied ☐   Medium-Bodied ☐   Full-Bodied ☐

Ageability:

Ready to drink? ☐   Needs more time? ☐   Past its prime? ☐

Cost: _____   Date Purchased: _____   Where Purchased: _____

Personal Ratings/Comments: _____

_____

_____

_____

Date: _____

TASTING NOTES

Country: _____   Region: _____   Vintage: _____   Producer: _____

60 Second Wine Tasting:

0-15 _____
_____

15-30 _____
_____

30-45 _____
_____

45-60 _____
_____

	Low	Medium	High
Residual Sugar			
Fruit			
Acid			
Tannin			

Color: _____

Aroma/Bouquet: _____
_____
_____
_____

Light-Bodied ☐   Medium-Bodied ☐   Full-Bodied ☐

Ageability:
Ready to drink? ☐   Needs more time? ☐   Past its prime? ☐

Cost: _____   Date Purchased: _____   Where Purchased: _____

Personal Ratings/Comments: _____
_____
_____
_____

Date: _____

TASTING NOTES

Country: _____   Region: _____   Vintage: _____   Producer: _____

60 Second Wine Tasting:

0-15 _____

_____

15-30 _____

30-45 _____

_____

45-60 _____

_____

	Low	Medium	High
Residual Sugar			
Fruit			
Acid			
Tannin			

Color: _____

Aroma/Bouquet: _____

_____

_____

_____

Light-Bodied ☐   Medium-Bodied ☐   Full-Bodied ☐

Ageability:
Ready to drink? ☐   Needs more time? ☐   Past its prime? ☐

Cost: _____   Date Purchased: _____   Where Purchased: _____

Personal Ratings/Comments: _____

_____

_____

Date: _____

TASTING NOTES

Country: _____ Region: _____ Vintage: _____ Producer: _____

60 Second Wine Tasting:

0-15 _____

_____

15-30 _____

_____

30-45 _____

_____

45-60 _____

_____

	Low	Medium	High
Residual Sugar			
Fruit			
Acid			
Tannin			

Color: _____

Aroma/Bouquet: _____

_____

_____

_____

Light-Bodied ☐   Medium-Bodied ☐   Full-Bodied ☐

Ageability:

Ready to drink? ☐   Needs more time? ☐   Past its prime? ☐

Cost: _____ Date Purchased: _____ Where Purchased: _____

Personal Ratings/Comments: _____

_____

_____

_____

Date: _____

TASTING NOTES

Country: _____   Region: _____   Vintage: _____   Producer: _____

60 Second Wine Tasting:

0-15 _____

_____

15-30 _____

_____

30-45 _____

_____

45-60 _____

_____

	Low	Medium	High
Residual Sugar			
Fruit			
Acid			
Tannin			

Color: _____

Aroma/Bouquet: _____

_____

_____

_____

Light-Bodied ☐   Medium-Bodied ☐   Full-Bodied ☐

Ageability:
Ready to drink? ☐   Needs more time? ☐   Past its prime? ☐

Cost: _____   Date Purchased: _____   Where Purchased: _____

Personal Ratings/Comments: _____

_____

_____

_____

Date: _____

TASTING NOTES

Country: _____ Region: _____ Vintage: _____ Producer: _____

60 Second Wine Tasting:

0-15 _____
_____

15-30 _____
_____

30-45 _____
_____

45-60 _____
_____

	Low	Medium	High
Residual Sugar			
Fruit			
Acid			
Tannin			

Color: _____

Aroma/Bouquet: _____
_____
_____

Light-Bodied ☐   Medium-Bodied ☐   Full-Bodied ☐

Ageability:
Ready to drink? ☐   Needs more time? ☐   Past its prime? ☐

Cost: _____ Date Purchased: _____ Where Purchased: _____

Personal Ratings/Comments: _____
_____
_____
_____

Date: _____

TASTING NOTES

Country: _____   Region: _____   Vintage: _____   Producer: _____

60 Second Wine Tasting:

0-15 _____

_____

15-30 _____

30-45 _____

_____

45-60 _____

_____

	Low	Medium	High
Residual Sugar			
Fruit			
Acid			
Tannin			

Color: _____

Aroma/Bouquet: _____

_____

_____

_____

Light-Bodied ☐   Medium-Bodied ☐   Full-Bodied ☐

Ageability:
Ready to drink? ☐   Needs more time? ☐   Past its prime? ☐

Cost: _____   Date Purchased: _____   Where Purchased: _____

Personal Ratings/Comments: _____

_____

_____

_____

Date: _____

TASTING NOTES

Country: _____   Region: _____   Vintage: _____   Producer: _____

60 Second Wine Tasting:

0-15 _____

_____

15-30 _____

_____

30-45 _____

_____

45-60 _____

_____

	Low	Medium	High
Residual Sugar			
Fruit			
Acid			
Tannin			

Color: _____

Aroma/Bouquet: _____

_____

_____

_____

Light-Bodied ☐   Medium-Bodied ☐   Full-Bodied ☐

Ageability:
Ready to drink? ☐   Needs more time? ☐   Past its prime? ☐

Cost: _____   Date Purchased: _____   Where Purchased: _____

Personal Ratings/Comments: _____

_____

_____

_____

Date: _____

TASTING NOTES

Country: _____ Region: _____ Vintage: _____ Producer: _____

60 Second Wine Tasting:

0-15 _____

_____

15-30 _____

_____

30-45 _____

_____

45-60 _____

_____

	Low	Medium	High
Residual Sugar			
Fruit			
Acid			
Tannin			

Color: _____

Aroma/Bouquet: _____

_____

_____

_____

Light-Bodied ☐   Medium-Bodied ☐   Full-Bodied ☐

Ageability:
Ready to drink? ☐   Needs more time? ☐   Past its prime? ☐

Cost: _____ Date Purchased: _____ Where Purchased: _____

Personal Ratings/Comments: _____

_____

_____

_____

Date: _____

TASTING NOTES

Country: _____   Region: _____   Vintage: _____   Producer: _____

60 Second Wine Tasting:

0-15 _____

_____

15-30 _____

_____

30-45 _____

_____

45-60 _____

_____

	Low	Medium	High
Residual Sugar			
Fruit			
Acid			
Tannin			

Color: _____

Aroma/Bouquet: _____

_____

_____

_____

Light-Bodied ☐   Medium-Bodied ☐   Full-Bodied ☐

Ageability:

Ready to drink? ☐   Needs more time? ☐   Past its prime? ☐

Cost: _____   Date Purchased: _____   Where Purchased: _____

Personal Ratings/Comments: _____

_____

_____

Date: _____

TASTING NOTES

Country: _____   Region: _____   Vintage: _____   Producer: _____

60 Second Wine Tasting:

0-15 _____

_____

15-30 _____

_____

30-45 _____

_____

45-60 _____

_____

	Low	Medium	High
Residual Sugar			
Fruit			
Acid			
Tannin			

Color: _____

Aroma/Bouquet: _____

_____

_____

_____

Light-Bodied ☐   Medium-Bodied ☐   Full-Bodied ☐

Ageability:
Ready to drink? ☐   Needs more time? ☐   Past its prime? ☐

Cost: _____   Date Purchased: _____   Where Purchased: _____

Personal Ratings/Comments: _____

_____

_____

_____

Date: _____

TASTING NOTES

Country: _____   Region: _____   Vintage: _____   Producer: _____

60 Second Wine Tasting:

0-15 _____

_____

15-30 _____

_____

30-45 _____

_____

45-60 _____

_____

	Low	Medium	High
Residual Sugar			
Fruit			
Acid			
Tannin			

Color: _____

Aroma/Bouquet: _____

_____

_____

_____

Light-Bodied ☐   Medium-Bodied ☐   Full-Bodied ☐

Ageability:
Ready to drink? ☐   Needs more time? ☐   Past its prime? ☐

Cost: _____   Date Purchased: _____   Where Purchased: _____

Personal Ratings/Comments: _____

_____

_____

_____

Date: _____

TASTING NOTES

Country: _____   Region: _____   Vintage: _____   Producer: _____

60 Second Wine Tasting:

0-15 _____

_____

15-30 _____

_____

30-45 _____

_____

45-60 _____

_____

	Low	Medium	High
Residual Sugar			
Fruit			
Acid			
Tannin			

Color: _____

Aroma/Bouquet: _____

_____

_____

_____

Light-Bodied ☐   Medium-Bodied ☐   Full-Bodied ☐

Ageability:
Ready to drink? ☐   Needs more time? ☐   Past its prime? ☐

Cost: _____   Date Purchased: _____   Where Purchased: _____

Personal Ratings/Comments: _____

_____

_____

_____

Date: _____

TASTING NOTES

Country: _____   Region: _____   Vintage: _____   Producer: _____

60 Second Wine Tasting:

0-15 _____
_____

15-30 _____
_____

30-45 _____
_____

45-60 _____
_____

	Low	Medium	High
Residual Sugar			
Fruit			
Acid			
Tannin			

Color: _____

Aroma/Bouquet: _____

_____

_____

_____

Light-Bodied ☐   Medium-Bodied ☐   Full-Bodied ☐

Ageability:

Ready to drink? ☐   Needs more time? ☐   Past its prime? ☐

Cost: _____   Date Purchased: _____   Where Purchased: _____

Personal Ratings/Comments: _____

_____

_____

_____

Date: _____

TASTING NOTES

Country: _____   Region: _____   Vintage: _____   Producer: _____

60 Second Wine Tasting:

0-15 _____

_____

15-30 _____

_____

30-45 _____

_____

45-60 _____

_____

	Low	Medium	High
Residual Sugar			
Fruit			
Acid			
Tannin			

Color: _____

Aroma/Bouquet: _____

_____

_____

_____

Light-Bodied ☐   Medium-Bodied ☐   Full-Bodied ☐

Ageability:
Ready to drink? ☐   Needs more time? ☐   Past its prime? ☐

Cost: _____   Date Purchased: _____   Where Purchased: _____

Personal Ratings/Comments: _____

_____

_____

_____

Date: _____

TASTING NOTES

Country: _____   Region: _____   Vintage: _____   Producer: _____

60 Second Wine Tasting:

0-15 _____

_____

15-30 _____

_____

30-45 _____

_____

45-60 _____

_____

	Low	Medium	High
Residual Sugar			
Fruit			
Acid			
Tannin			

Color: _____

Aroma/Bouquet: _____

_____

_____

_____

Light-Bodied ☐   Medium-Bodied ☐   Full-Bodied ☐

Ageability:
Ready to drink? ☐   Needs more time? ☐   Past its prime? ☐

Cost: _____   Date Purchased: _____   Where Purchased: _____

Personal Ratings/Comments: _____

_____

_____

_____

Date: _____

TASTING NOTES

Country: _____   Region: _____   Vintage: _____   Producer: _____

60 Second Wine Tasting:

0-15 _____

_____

15-30 _____

_____

30-45 _____

_____

45-60 _____

_____

	Low	Medium	High
Residual Sugar			
Fruit			
Acid			
Tannin			

Color: _____

Aroma/Bouquet: _____

_____

_____

_____

Light-Bodied ☐   Medium-Bodied ☐   Full-Bodied ☐

Ageability:
Ready to drink? ☐   Needs more time? ☐   Past its prime? ☐

Cost: _____   Date Purchased: _____   Where Purchased: _____

Personal Ratings/Comments: _____

_____

_____

_____

Date: _____

WINE LABELS

TASTING NOTES

Country: _____   Region: _____   Vintage: _____   Producer: _____

60 Second Wine Tasting:

0-15 _____

_____

15-30 _____

_____

30-45 _____

_____

45-60 _____

_____

	Low	Medium	High
Residual Sugar			
Fruit			
Acid			
Tannin			

Color: _____

Aroma/Bouquet: _____

_____

_____

_____

Light-Bodied ☐   Medium-Bodied ☐   Full-Bodied ☐

Ageability:
Ready to drink? ☐   Needs more time? ☐   Past its prime? ☐

Cost: _____   Date Purchased: _____   Where Purchased: _____

Personal Ratings/Comments: _____

_____

_____

_____

Date: _____

WINE LABELS

TASTING NOTES

Country: _____   Region: _____   Vintage: _____   Producer: _____

60 Second Wine Tasting:

0-15 _____

_____

15-30 _____

_____

30-45 _____

_____

45-60 _____

_____

	Low	Medium	High
Residual Sugar			
Fruit			
Acid			
Tannin			

Color: _____

Aroma/Bouquet: _____

_____

_____

_____

Light-Bodied ☐   Medium-Bodied ☐   Full-Bodied ☐

Ageability:
Ready to drink? ☐   Needs more time? ☐   Past its prime? ☐

Cost: _____   Date Purchased: _____   Where Purchased: _____

Personal Ratings/Comments: _____

_____

_____

_____

Date: _____

TASTING NOTES

Country: _____ Region: _____ Vintage: _____ Producer: _____

60 Second Wine Tasting:

0-15 _____

_____

15-30 _____

_____

30-45 _____

_____

45-60 _____

_____

	Low	Medium	High
Residual Sugar			
Fruit			
Acid			
Tannin			

Color: _____

Aroma/Bouquet: _____

_____

_____

_____

Light-Bodied ☐   Medium-Bodied ☐   Full-Bodied ☐

Ageability:
Ready to drink? ☐   Needs more time? ☐   Past its prime? ☐

Cost: _____ Date Purchased: _____ Where Purchased: _____

Personal Ratings/Comments: _____

_____

_____

_____

Date: _____